CENTRAL ARKANSAS
NATIONAL WILDLIFE REFUGE COMPLEX

Comprehensive Conservation Plan

U.S. Department of the Interior
Fish and Wildlife Service
Southeast Region

October 2009

Submitted by: _____   *Date:* 12/1/09
                 for Keith Weaver, Project Leader
        Central Arkansas National Wildlife Refuge Complex

Concur: _____   *Date:* 12/28/09
                 Ricky Ingram, Refuge Supervisor
                              Southeast Region

Concur: _____   *Date:* 12/28/09
                 Jon Andrew, Regional Chief
                              Southeast Region

Approved by: _____   *Date:* 12/28/09
                 Cynthia Dohner, Regional Director
                              Southeast Region

COMPREHENSIVE CONSERVATION PLAN

CENTRAL ARKANSAS NATIONAL WILDLIFE REFUGE COMPLEX
Bald Knob, Big Lake, Cache River, and Wapanocca National Wildlife Refuges

U.S. Department of the Interior
Fish and Wildlife Service

Southeast Region
Atlanta, Georgia

October 2009

TABLE OF CONTENTS

COMPREHENSIVE CONSERVATION PLAN

EXECUTIVE SUMMARY 1

I. BACKGROUND..3

    Introduction..3
    Purpose and Need for Plan 3
    Fish and Wildlife Service 4
    National Wildlife Refuge System 4
    Legal Policy Context...4
        National Wildlife Refuge System Improvement Act of 1997....................................4
    National and International Conservation Priorities and Initiatives 5
        North American Waterfowl Management Plan...6
        Partners In Flight Bird Conservation Plan 6
        United States Shorebird Conservation Plan...7
        Fisheries Vision for the Future 7
        American Woodcock Management Plan 7
        North American Waterbird Conservation Plan 7
    Relationship to State Wildlife Agency...8

II. REFUGE OVERVIEW..9

    Introduction...9
    Refuge History and Purpose 9
        Bald Knob National Wildlife Refuge 9
        Big Lake National Wildlife Refuge..11
        Cache River National Wildlife Refuge 11
        Wapanocca National Wildlife Refuge 12
    Special Designations 12
    Ecosystem Context...13
        Overview 13
        Lower Mississippi River Ecosystem Priorities 13
    Regional Conservation Plans and Initiatives 15
        The Big Woods of Arkansas...15
        Arkansas Wildlife Action Plan 15
    Ecological Threats and Problems...15
        Climate...16
        Soils 17
        Hydrology...17
        Water Quality and Quantity 22
    Biological Resources 23
        Habitat...23
    Cultural Resources 39
    Socioeconomic Environment 41
    Refuge Administration and Management 42
        Visitor Services 42
        Personnel, Operations, and Maintenance 53

III. PLAN DEVELOPMENT 55

Summary of Issues, Concerns, and Opportunities 55

IV. MANAGEMENT DIRECTION 63
    Introduction 63
    Vision 63
    Goals, Objectives, and Strategies 63
    Bald Knob National wildlife refuge..64
        Fish and Wildlife Population Management..64
        Habitat Management...79
        Resource Protection 87
        Visitor Services 92
        Refuge Administration 103
    Big Lake National Wildlife Refuge 107
        Fish and Wildlife Population Management..107
        Habitat Management...115
        Resource Protection 120
        Visitor Services 124
        Refuge Administration 132
    Cache River National Wildlife Refuge 136
        Fish and Wildlife Population Management..136
        Habitat Management...156
        Resource Protection 168
        Visitor Services 177
        Refuge Administration 186
    Wapanocca National Wildlife Refuge 190
        Fish and Wildlife Population Management..190
        Habitat Management...200
        Resource Protection 206
        Visitor Services 210
        Refuge Administration 219

V. PLAN IMPLEMENTATION 223
    Introduction 223
    Proposed Projects..223
        Fish and Wildlife Population Management..223
        Habitat Management...227
        Resource Protection 232
        Visitor Services 234
        Refuge Administration 243
    Funding and Personnel 250
    Step-Down Management Plans...253
    Monitoring and Adaptive Management..255
    Plan Review and Revision 255

APPENDICES

APPENDIX A. GLOSSARY 257

    ACRONYMS AND ABBREVIATIONS 264

APPENDIX B. REFERENCES AND LITERATURE CITATIONS................................267

APPENDIX C. RELEVANT LEGAL MANDATES AND EXECUTIVE ORDERS...........271

APPENDIX D. APPROPRIATE USE DETERMINATIONS 283

APPENDIX E. COMPATIBILITY DETERMINATIONS 333

APPENDIX F. INTRA-SERVICE SECTION 7 BIOLOGICAL EVALUATION...............455

APPENDIX G. REFUGE BIOTA...477

APPENDIX H. BIRDS OF CONSERVATION CONCERN FOR BCR 26 OCCURRING
ON CENTRAL ARKANSAS NWR COMPLEX..497

APPENDIX I. BUDGET REQUESTS...499

    REFUGE OPERATING NEEDS SYSTEM (RONS) 499
    SERVICE ASSET MAINTENANCE MANAGEMENT SYSTEM (SAMMS)...........500

APPENDIX J. WILDERNESS REVIEW 505

APPENDIX K. PUBLIC INVOLVEMENT, CONSULTATION, COORDINATION,
AND COMMENTS 507

    SUMMARY OF PUBLIC SCOPING IN THE PLANNING PROCESS 507
    SUMMARY OF DRAFT CCP/EA PUBLIC COMMENTS AND SERVICE RESPONSES 509

APPENDIX L. LIST OF PREPARERS 513

    PLANNING TEAM 513
    CONTRIBUTORS 514

APPENDIX M. FINDING OF NO SIGNIFICANT IMPACT..517

    INTRODUCTION 517
    ALTERNATIVES...517
        Alternative A – Maintain Current Management (No Action Alternative) 517
        Alternative B – Minimal Management Alternative 517
        Alternative C – Enhanced Habitat Management and Public Use Programs (Preferred
        Alternative) 518
    SELECTION RATIONALE..518
    ENVIRONMENTAL EFFECTS 518
    POTENTIAL ADVERSE EFFECTS AND MITIGATION MEASURES 519
        Wildlife Disturbance 519
        Vegetation Disturbance...520
        User Group Conflicts 520
        Effects on Adjacent Landowners..520

LAND OWNERSHIP AND SITE DEVELOPMENT...520
COORDINATION 521
FINDINGS 521
SUPPORTING REFERENCES 522
DOCUMENT AVAILABILITY...523

LIST OF FIGURES

Figure 1. Central Arkansas NWR Complex 10
Figure 2. Location of Central Arkansas NWR Complex in the LMRE 14
Figure 3. Forest Types on Bald Knob NWR...24
Figure 4. Habitat Types on Big Lake NWR 26
Figure 5a. Forest Types on Cache River NWR (North) 28
Figure 5b. Forest Types on Cache River NWR (South).......................................29
Figure 6. Habitat Types on Wapanocca NWR 30
Figure 7. Proposed Minimal Disturbance Zone for Waterfowl on Bald Knob NWR 97

LIST OF TABLES

Table 1. Hunting opportunities offered at Bald Knob NWR for the 2008-09 season..........................44
Table 2. Hunting opportunities offered at Big Lake NWR for the 2009-09 season 45
Table 3. Hunter participation and harvest data for Big Lake NWR's 2008-09 season.......................46
Table 4. Hunting opportunities offered at Cache River NWR for the 2008-09 season......................48
Table 5. Hunting opportunities offered at Wapanocca NWR for the 2008-09 season 50
Table 6. Hunter participation and harvest information for Wapanocca NWR's 2007-08 season..51
Table 7. Bald Knob NWR - Current migrating and wintering waterfowl foraging habitat objectives 65
Table 8. Carrying capacity of selected foraging habitats of dabbling ducks wintering in the LMRJV[1] 66
Table 9. Big Lake NWR - Current migrating and wintering waterfowl foraging habitat objectives 109
Table 10. Cache River NWR - Current migrating and wintering waterfowl foraging habitat objectives 138
Table 11. Hypothesized forest area required to support viable populations of 500 breeding birds within the MAV 143
Table 12. Wapanocca NWR - Current migrating and wintering waterfowl foraging habitat objectives 191
Table 13. Summary of Projects..246
Table 14. Central Arkansas National Wildlife Refuge Complex step-down management plans 254

Executive Summary

The U.S. Fish and Wildlife Service (Service) has prepared this Comprehensive Conservation Plan (CCP) to guide the management of the Central Arkansas National Wildlife Refuge (NWR) Complex (Complex). The Complex is comprised of Bald Knob, Big Lake, Cache River, and Wapanocca NWRs that are located in Crittenden, Jackson, Mississippi, Monroe, Prairie, White, and Woodruff Counties of east and central Arkansas. The CCP outlines programs and corresponding resource needs for the next 15 years, as mandated by the National Wildlife Refuge System Improvement Act of 1997.

Before the Service began planning, it conducted biological and public use reviews of the refuge's management programs and conducted public scoping meetings to solicit public opinion of the issues the plan should address. The biological review teams were composed of biologists from federal and state agencies and non-governmental organizations that have an interest in the refuge. The public use review teams consisted of visitor services managers from selected refuges in the southeast. These diverse teams presented the Service with refuge management recommendations regarding habitat, wildlife, natural resources (e.g., water, timber, oil and gas), cultural resources, administration, and visitor services. Additionally, the Complex staff held five public scoping meetings to solicit public opinion of the issues that the plan should address.

A planning team comprised of Service personnel, state agency representatives, non-governmental organizations, and others then developed an Environmental Assessment that analyzed a range of alternatives for refuge management that the Service would reasonably undertake to achieve the goals and fulfill the purposes of the refuges. Three possible alternatives (Alternatives A, B, and C) emerged for consideration and were provided in the Draft Comprehensive Conservation Plan and Environmental Assessment. A 30-day public review and comment period was provided and five public meetings were held to solicit public opinion of the proposed alternative. All input received from the public during the planning process was carefully considered during the development of this CCP.

Under Alternative A, the "No Action" Alternative, management on the Complex would not change, but would continue the current actions and direction on the Central Arkansas NWR Complex. The Complex would continue to restore, protect, and manage bottomland hardwood forests, wetlands, cropland units, moist-soil units, open water areas, grassland/scrub-shrub areas, and the Big Lake Wilderness. Management activities would continue to focus on afforestation and reforestation, restoration of wetlands, invasive plant and nuisance animal management, cooperative farming, inventorying and monitoring, and priority public uses (hunting, fishing, wildlife observation, wildlife photography, and environmental education and interpretation). The refuges would continue to acquire land from willing sellers and expand but only within the approved acquisition boundaries.

Under Alternative B, the "Minimal Management" Alternative, the Complex would undertake minimal wildlife, habitat, and infrastructure management. In this "let nature take its course" alternative, there would be no more active reforestation efforts, no moist-soil impoundments and croplands, and no more road, beaver dam, or invasive species management and maintenance programs. Natural succession would be allowed to proceed unchecked, providing for development of early stage or successional forest habitat on abandoned lands, and no silvicultural treatments in existing forest stands would be conducted. All refuges would implement a custodial or passive stewardship approach to management and would monitor natural succession and wildlife populations over time. Quality and quantity of habitats for wildlife would be expected to decline along with wildlife use of these habitats. There would likely be reduced associated public use because roadways and facilities would not be maintained and the quality of visitor services would diminish. There would be no change in the acreage or amount of waterfowl sanctuaries. The refuges would acquire land from willing sellers, but only within the approved acquisition boundaries.

By implementing Alternative C, the "Preferred" Alternative, the Complex would actively expand and improve habitat management and public use programs. The refuges would intensify and enhance forest, moist-soil, scrub-shrub, grassland, and aquatic management programs in order to increase benefits for waterfowl, shorebirds, water birds, other migratory birds, and other species of native wildlife. Hydrologic, wetland, and forest restoration projects would also be expanded. Invasive plant and animal control projects would be increased. A full range of inventorying, monitoring, and research programs would be developed and implemented to enable adaptive management. Habitat conservation and restoration would continue and expand through land acquisition projects from willing sellers, but boundary expansions would also be pursued. Environmental education and interpretive programs would be improved as part of a comprehensive visitor services program. Opportunities for hunting, fishing, and wildlife observation would be expanded, and law enforcement coverage would be increased for more effective protection of resources and visitors. Additional staff would be recruited, additional equipment would be acquired, and improved facilities would be installed to enable implementation of these projects and programs.

The Service selected Alternative C, the "Preferred Alternative," as the CCP for guiding the management of the four refuges within the Complex for the next 15 years, because it directs the development of programs to best achieve the vision of the Complex and each refuge's purposes and goals; emphasizes improvements to the capacity and capability of the refuges to better manage the habitat and wildlife resources as well as expand visitor services and public use programs; collects habitat and wildlife data; and ensures long-term achievement of refuge and Service objectives. At the same time, these management actions provide balanced levels of compatible public use opportunities consistent with existing laws, Service policies, and sound biological principles.

Under this alternative, all lands under the management and direction of the Complex will be protected, maintained, and enhanced to best achieve national, ecosystem, and refuge-specific goals and objectives within anticipated funding and staffing levels. In addition, the action positively addresses significant issues and concerns expressed by the public.

The overriding concern reflected in this CCP is that wildlife conservation assumes first priority in refuge management; wildlife-dependent recreational uses are allowed if they are compatible with wildlife conservation. Wildlife-dependent recreation uses (hunting, fishing, wildlife observation, wildlife photography, and environmental education and interpretation) will be emphasized and encouraged.

This CCP provides the best mix of program elements to achieve desired long-term conditions.

I. Background

INTRODUCTION

This Comprehensive Conservation Plan (CCP) for the Central Arkansas National Wildlife Refuge (NWR) Complex (Complex), which includes the refuges of Bald Knob, Big Lake, Cache River, and Wapanocca, was prepared to guide management actions and direction for the refuges over the next 15 years. Fish and wildlife conservation will receive first priority in management of the refuges, while wildlife-dependent recreation will be allowed and encouraged as long as it is compatible with, and does not detract from, the mission of the National Wildlife Refuge System (Refuge System) or the purposes for which the refuges were established.

A planning team comprised of U.S. Fish and Wildlife Service (Service) personnel, state wildlife agency representatives, non-governmental organizations, and others developed a range of alternatives for refuge management that the Service could reasonably undertake to achieve the goals and fulfill the purposes for each refuge in the Complex. These alternatives were presented in the Draft Comprehensive Conservation Plan/Environmental Assessment (Draft CCP/EA) that described the proposed alternatives that were considered and their effects on the environment. Each alternative consisted of different sets of goals, objectives, and strategies for management of the refuges.

The Draft CCP/EA was made available to state and federal government agencies, conservation partners, and the general public for review and comment from August 27, 2009, through

September 28, 2009. Comments from each entity were carefully considered in the development of this CCP.

PURPOSE AND NEED FOR PLAN

The purpose of the CCP is to ensure that each refuge contributes to the National Wildlife Refuge System's (Refuge System) mission to provide a network of lands and waters for the conservation, management, and where appropriate, restoration of the fish, wildlife, and plant resources and their habitats within the United States for the benefit of present and future generations of Americans.

Specifically, the CCP is needed to:

- provide a clear statement of management direction for the refuges;

- provide refuge neighbors, visitors, and government officials with an understanding of Service management actions on and around the refuges;

- ensure that Service management actions, including land protection, recreation, and education programs, are consistent with the mandates of the Refuge System;

- ensure that refuge management is consistent with the purposes for which the refuges were established;

- ensure that refuge management is consistent with federal, state, and local plans and contributes to the Service's ecosystem management goals for the ecosystem in which the refuges are located; and

- provide a basis for the development of budget requests for operations, maintenance, and capital improvement needs.

FISH AND WILDLIFE SERVICE

The Service is the primary federal agency responsible for conserving, protecting, and enhancing the Nation's fish and wildlife resources and their habitats. The mission of the Service is "working with others to conserve, protect, and enhance fish, wildlife, and plants and their habitats for the continuing benefit of the American people."

Responsibilities are shared with other federal, state, tribal, and local entities; however, the Service has specific responsibilities for endangered species, migratory birds, inter-jurisdictional fish, and certain marine mammals, as well as for lands and waters administered by the Service for the management and protection of these resources. It also operates national fish hatcheries, fishery resource offices, and ecological services field stations. The Service enforces federal wildlife laws; administers the Endangered Species Act; manages migratory bird populations; restores nationally significant fisheries; conserves and restores wildlife habitat, such as wetlands; and helps foreign governments with their conservation efforts. It also oversees the Federal Aid Program that distributes hundreds of millions of dollars from excise taxes on fishing and hunting equipment to state fish and wildlife agencies.

NATIONAL WILDLIFE REFUGE SYSTEM

The mission of the Refuge System is "...to administer a national network of lands and waters for the conservation, management, and where appropriate, restoration of the fish, wildlife, and plant resources and their habitats within the United States for the benefit of present and future generations of Americans."

The Service manages the 95-million-acre Refuge System, which encompasses over 545 national wildlife refuges, thousands of small wetlands, and other special management areas. The majority of these lands, 77 million acres, is in Alaska, with the remaining acres located among the other 49 states and several territories. Approximately 82 million acres in the Refuge System were reserved from the public domain. The remainder was acquired through purchase, from other federal agencies, as gifts, or through easement and lease agreements.

LEGAL POLICY CONTEXT

The mission and goals of the Refuge System, congressional legislation, presidential executive orders, and international treaties guide administration of national wildlife refuges. Policies for management options of refuges are defined in administrative guidelines established by the Secretary of the Interior and by policy guidelines established by the Director of the Fish and Wildlife Service. Refer to Appendix C for a complete listing of relevant legal mandates.

NATIONAL WILDLIFE REFUGE SYSTEM IMPROVEMENT ACT OF 1997

An important milestone occurred in 1997, with the passage of the National Wildlife Refuge System Improvement Act (Improvement Act), which has been called the "Organic Act" of the Refuge System.

The Improvement Act established, for the first time, a clear legislative mission of wildlife conservation for the Refuge System.

The Improvement Act also recognized the outstanding recreational opportunities on refuges. The Refuge System has long provided some of the Nation's best hunting and fishing, and our refuges continue to support these deeply rooted American traditions. The law identified and established compatible wildlife-dependent recreation (e.g., hunting, fishing, wildlife observation, wildlife photography, and environmental education and interpretation) as priority public uses of the Refuge System. Among other things, this far-reaching law required comprehensive conservation planning for each refuge, and set standards to assure that all uses of refuges are compatible with their purposes and the Refuge System's wildlife conservation mission. It also required the Service to conserve the biological integrity, diversity, and environmental health of refuges, and consider the conservation of the ecosystems of the United States, while planning the growth of the Refuge System.

The Service's planning process is premised on strong partnerships with state fish and wildlife agencies. It provides an opportunity to use sound science in managing refuges, thereby assuring an ecological perspective of how refuges fit into the greater surrounding landscapes. The planning process also provides citizens with a meaningful role in shaping the future management of refuges and recognizes the important role that refuges play in the lives of nearby communities.

The Improvement Act states that each refuge shall be managed to:

- fulfill the mission of the Refuge System;

- fulfill the individual purpose(s) of each refuge;

- consider the needs of wildlife first;

- fulfill requirements of comprehensive conservation plans that are prepared for each unit of the Refuge System;

- maintain the biological integrity, diversity, and environmental health of the Refuge System;

- recognize that wildlife-dependent recreation activities, including hunting, fishing, wildlife observation, wildlife photography, and environmental education and interpretation, are legitimate and priority public uses; and

- allow refuge managers authority to determine compatible public uses.

NATIONAL AND INTERNATIONAL CONSERVATION PRIORITIES AND INITIATIVES

Conservation priorities for national wildlife refuges in the Lower Mississippi Valley focus on threatened and endangered species, trust species, and species of local concern. Goals and objectives in this CCP are stepped-down from the following plans:

- North American Waterfowl Management Plan;

- Partners in Flight Bird Conservation Plan;

- North American Bird Conservation Initiative;

- United States Shorebird Conservation Plan;

- Fisheries Vision for the Future;

- American Woodcock Management Plan.

NORTH AMERICAN WATERFOWL MANAGEMENT PLAN

The North American Waterfowl Management Plan (NAWMP), signed by the United States and Canadian governments in 1986, undertook an intensive effort to protect and restore North America's waterfowl populations and their habitats. With its update in 1994, Mexico became a signatory to the plan. Restoration of wetlands and associated ecosystems is the main premise of the plan in order to restore waterfowl populations to levels observed in the 1970s.

Refuges within the Complex provide important foraging and resting habitats (e.g., sanctuaries) for waterfowl and serve an integral role in a large, cooperative planning and habitat management effort.

PARTNERS IN FLIGHT BIRD CONSERVATION PLAN

The National Fish and Wildlife Foundation led efforts in the 1990s to form the Partners in Flight program that combines resources and knowledge to protect the natural diversity of our continent. Many partners have made the program successful by participating in Working Groups to develop Regional Bird Conservation Plans that set conservation priorities and habitat and population objectives.

The Complex's refuges are located within Physiographic Area 5 and can contribute to the plan's actions for restoration projects to benefit migratory landbirds. Habitats found on the refuges and those associated bird focal species that use them are:

- Bottomland hardwood forests – Ivory-billed Woodpecker, Swallow-tailed Kite, Swainson's Warbler, Cerulean Warbler, Prothonotary Warbler, and Northern Parula;

- Secondary growth – Painted Bunting and Bell's Vireo;

- Moist-soils and croplands – shorebirds and waterfowl.

NORTH AMERICAN BIRD CONSERVATION INITIATIVE

This initiative is a broad coalition of governmental, non-governmental, and academic organizations interested in coordinating efforts to conserve bird populations and the landscapes upon which they depend. It evolved in 1998, when conservationists recognized the value of coordinating and integrating planning, implementation, and evaluation efforts associated with the North American Waterfowl Management Plan, Partners in Flight, U.S. Shorebird Conservation Plan, and the North American Waterbird Conservation Plan.

UNITED STATES SHOREBIRD CONSERVATION PLAN

The United States Shorebird Conservation Plan is a partnership involving organizations throughout the United States committed to the conservation of shorebirds. Primary objectives of this plan are to:

- develop a scientifically sound monitoring system to provide practical information to researchers and land managers;

- identify principles upon which management plans can integrate shorebird habitat conservation with multiple species strategies;

- design a strategy for increasing public awareness and information concerning wetlands and shorebirds.

The refuges within the Complex are included in the Lower Mississippi/Western Gulf Coast Shorebird Region. The plan recommends that public lands provide as much fall shorebird habitat as possible to meet the goal of 5,000 acres of fall habitat in Arkansas. In this plan, bird species that should be considered a high priority for the refuges include: Piping Plover, American Golden-plover, Marbled Godwit, Ruddy Turnstone, Red Knot, Sanderling, Buff-breasted Sandpiper, American Woodcock, and Wilson's Phalarope.

FISHERIES VISION FOR THE FUTURE

In 2001, the Service worked with partners to refocus its Fisheries Program and develop a vision. This vision of the Service and its Fisheries Program is *"working with partners to restore and maintain fish and other aquatic resources at self-sustaining levels and to support Federal mitigation programs for the benefit of the American public."*

To achieve the vision, the Fisheries Program works with its partners to:

- protect the health of aquatic habitats;

- restore fish and other aquatic resources; and

- provide opportunities to enjoy the benefits of healthy aquatic resources.

AMERICAN WOODCOCK MANAGEMENT PLAN

The American Woodcock Management Plan sets management goals to restore woodcock population to levels consistent with the demands of consumptive and non-consumptive users (U.S. Fish and Wildlife Service 1990). Reliable annual population estimates, harvest estimates, and information on recruitment and distribution are essential for comprehensive woodcock management, as well as conserving and managing habitat. No step-down management plans have been written, but the plan provides general guidance for habitat and population management at the national level.

NORTH AMERICAN WATERBIRD CONSERVATION PLAN

This plan provides a framework for the conservation and management of 210 species of waterbirds in 29 nations. Threats to waterbird populations include destruction of inland and coastal wetlands, introduced predators and invasive species, pollutants, mortality from fisheries and industries, disturbance, and conflicts arising from abundant species. Particularly important habitats of the southeast region include pelagic areas, marshes, forested wetlands, and barrier and sea island complexes. Fifteen species of waterbirds are federally listed including breeding populations of Wood Storks, Mississippi Sandhill Cranes, Whooping Cranes, Interior Least Terns, and Gulf Coast populations of Brown Pelicans (Hunter and Golder, In prep). A key objective of this plan is the standardization of data collection efforts to better recommend effective conservation measures.

RELATIONSHIP TO STATE WILDLIFE AGENCY

A provision of the Improvement Act, and subsequent agency policy, is that the Service shall ensure timely and effective cooperation and collaboration with other federal agencies and state fish and wildlife agencies during the course of acquiring and managing refuges. State wildlife management areas and national wildlife refuges provide the foundation for protection of species, and contribute to the overall health and diversity of fish and wildlife species in Arkansas.

The Arkansas Game and Fish Commission (AGFC) is the state fish and wildlife agency partnering with the Service. The AGFC plays an important role in keeping "The Natural State" true to its title. The agency is responsible for the protection, conservation, and preservation of fish and wildlife in Arkansas. This is done through habitat management, fish stocking, hunting and fishing regulations, and a host of other programs conducive to helping Arkansas' wildlife flourish. The AGFC manages over 280,000 acres of state-owned natural areas and wildlife management areas.

The state's participation and contribution throughout this planning process provides for open dialogue with the Service and continued opportunity to improve the ecological health and diversity of fish and wildlife in Arkansas. A vital part of the planning process is integrating common mission objectives, where appropriate.

II. Refuge Overview

INTRODUCTION

REFUGE HISTORY AND PURPOSE

The Central Arkansas NWR Complex is comprised of four refuges: Bald Knob, Big Lake, Cache River and Wapanocca, in east and central Arkansas (Figure 1). The Complex is supervised by a project leader and assisted by other staff located at the Cache River NWR. Additionally, each refuge has specific staff stationed on site.

BALD KNOB NATIONAL WILDLIFE REFUGE

Bald Knob NWR, located near the small town of Bald Knob in White County, Arkansas, was established in 1993, to protect and provide feeding and resting areas for migrating waterfowl. The Service's Final Environmental Assessment and land protection plan for the refuge stated the purpose for acquisition *"is for preservation of winter habitat for lesser-snow geese, Canada geese, mallards, pintail, blue-winged teal and wood ducks."* Annually, the refuge hosts the largest populations of wintering pintail in the state and is a crucial staging area for pintail migrating to the coastal areas of Louisiana and eastern Texas.

The refuge encompasses more than 15,000 acres of forested wetlands and croplands, located along the Little Red River and adjacent to the AGFC Henry Gray/Hurricane Lake Wildlife Management Area (WMA). Most of the refuge is flat or characterized by gentle ridges and swales. The refuge is an important link in protecting wildlife and habitat. One unit of the refuge is situated 3 miles west of the confluence of the Little Red River and the White River. These rivers are key water sources for the refuge.

Management activities on the refuge include cooperative farming to provide high energy foods (e.g., rice, milo, and millet for migratory birds), moist-soil development, installing and maintaining water control structures, restoring bottomland hardwood forests, and providing compatible wildlife-dependent recreation.

Bald Knob NWR's official purposes are:

"...the conservation of the wetlands of the Nation in order to maintain the public benefits they provide and to help fulfill international obligations contained in various migratory bird treaties and conventions..." 16 U.S.C. 3901(b) (Emergency Wetlands Resources Act of 1986).

"...for the development, advancement, management, conservation, and protection of fish and wildlife resources..." 16 U.S.C. 742f(a)(4) ...for the benefit of the United States Fish and Wildlife Service, in performing its activities and services. Such acceptance may be subject to the terms of any restrictive or affirmative covenant, or condition of servitude..." 16 U.S.C. 742f(b)(1) (Fish and Wildlife Act of 1956).

"...for use as an inviolate sanctuary, or for any other management purposes, for migratory birds." 16 U.S.C. 715d (Migratory Bird Conservation Act).

Figure 1. Central Arkansas NWR Complex

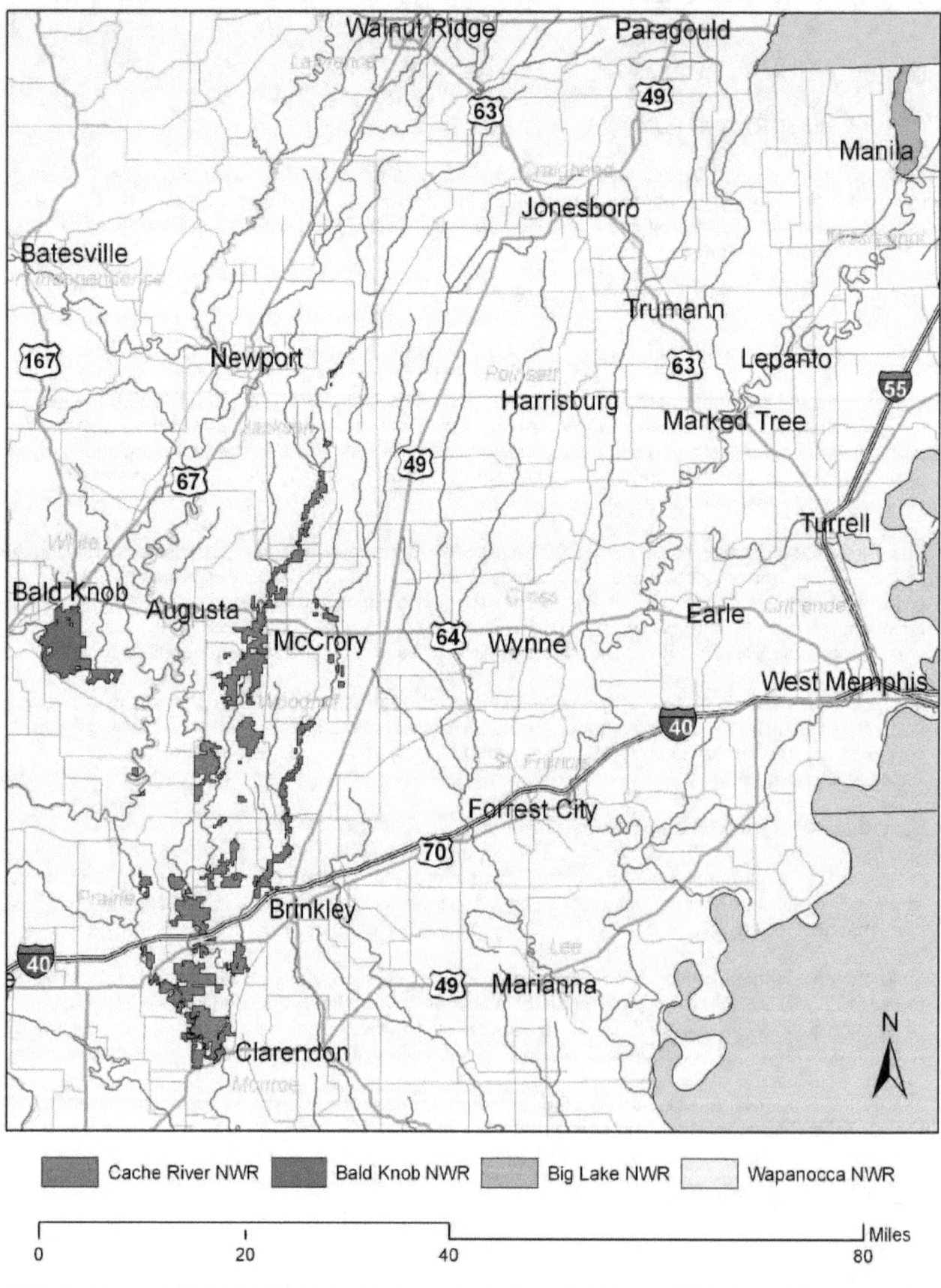

Cache River NWR   Bald Knob NWR   Big Lake NWR   Wapanocca NWR

			Miles
0	20	40	80

BIG LAKE NATIONAL WILDLIFE REFUGE

Big Lake NWR, located near the town of Manila in Mississippi County, Arkansas, was established in August 1915, by Executive Order of President Woodrow Wilson, to serve as a reserve and breeding ground for native birds. It is one of the Nation's oldest inland refuges and encompasses 11,038 acres. The New Madrid earthquakes of 1811 – 1812 changed the Big Lake area from a free-flowing river system to its present lake/swamp environment. An extensive network of ditches in the Missouri bootheel drains approximately 2,500 square miles of farmland directly through the refuge.

Big Lake NWR also administers two Farm Service Agency tracts and one conservation easement. The French Tract is located in Greene and Lawrence Counties and contains 108 acres. The French easement is also located in Greene County and encompasses 18 acres. The Craighead tract is located in Craighead County and contains 42 acres.

Management activities target water, waterfowl, wetland, forestry, wilderness stewardship, and compatible wildlife-dependent recreation.

Big Lake NWR's official purposes are:

"...as a refuge, reserve, and breeding ground for native birds" (Executive Order 2230, dated August 2, 1915).

"...for use as an inviolate sanctuary, or for any other management purposes, for migratory birds. " 16 U.S.C. 715d (Migratory Bird Conservation Act).

To manage the Big Lake Wilderness as part of the National Wilderness Preservation System according to the Wilderness Act of 1964, as compatible with the purposes for which Big Lake NWR was established.

CACHE RIVER NATIONAL WILDLIFE REFUGE

Cache River NWR, located in Jackson, Monroe, Prairie, and Woodruff Counties, in central Arkansas, was established on June 16, 1986, with the purchase of 1,395 acres. Land acquisition has continued on a willing-seller basis, and the refuge now includes more than 65,000 acres. The approved land acquisition boundary of 185,574 acres is defined as lands within the 10-year floodplain of the lower and middle Cache River Basin, including Bayou DeView.

The establishment of Cache River NWR exemplifies the Service's commitment to conserve and restore bottomland hardwood habitat in the Mississippi Alluvial Valley (MAV). The refuge features some of the largest remaining tracts of bottomland hardwood forest within the MAV. This unique complex of wetlands provides critical wintering habitat for waterfowl and other migratory and resident wildlife species.

Management activities focus on water, waterfowl, wetland, cropland, and forestry programs, and providing compatible wildlife-dependent recreation.

Cache River NWR's official purposes are:

"...the conservation of the wetlands of the Nation in order to maintain the public benefits they provide and to help fulfill international obligations contained in various migratory bird treaties and conventions..." 16 U.S.C. 3901(b) (Emergency Wetlands Resources Act of 1986).

"...for the development, advancement, management, conservation, and protection of fish and wildlife resources..." 16 U.S.C. 742f(a)(4) ...for the benefit of the United States Fish and Wildlife Service, in performing its activities and services. Such acceptance may be subject to the terms of any restrictive or affirmative covenant, or condition of servitude..." 16 U.S.C. 742f(b)(1) (Fish and Wildlife Act of 1956).

"...for use as an inviolate sanctuary, or for any other management purposes, for migratory birds." 16 U.S.C. 715d (Migratory Bird Conservation Act).

WAPANOCCA NATIONAL WILDLIFE REFUGE

Wapanocca NWR was established on January 24, 1961, with the leasing of 3,119 acres from the Wapanocca Outing Club. On January 1, 1966, another 1,695 acres was added to the refuge. Currently, the refuge totals 5,620 acres and is located 20 miles northwest of Memphis, Tennessee, in Crittenden County, Arkansas.

The refuge also administers two Farm Service Agency fee title tracts in St. Francis County. The Round Pond Unit contains 480 acres and the Pigmon Unit contains over 29 acres.

Wapanocca Lake is an oxbow lake formed when the Mississippi main channel changed its course. Subsequent flooding has deposited 5 to 6 feet of silt, creating what is now a shallow lake system. The refuge now remains as an island of wildlife habitat amidst a sea of agriculture. Habitat diversity includes agricultural land, grassland, bottomland hardwood forest, and flooded cypress/willow swamp.

The refuge provides a wintering area for migratory waterfowl, a nesting habitat for resident wood ducks, and as a link in the chain of refuges along the Mississippi River to accommodate the southward migration of Canada geese.

Management activities include water, waterfowl, wetland, cropland, and forestry management, and providing compatible wildlife-dependent recreation.

Wapanocca NWR's official purpose is:

"...for use as an inviolate sanctuary, or for any other management purposes, for migratory birds." 16 U.S.C. 715d (Migratory Bird Conservation Act).

SPECIAL DESIGNATIONS

Bald Knob NWR has been named as an "Important Birding Area" by the Audubon Arkansas Board of Directors.

Big Lake NWR contains about 5,000 acres of lands designated as a National Natural Landmark Area in the mid-1970s. The tract includes seasonally flooded bottomlands, open water, and permanently flooded swamplands. Pure stands of bald cypress, the only significant stands of virgin timber in the area, dominate the overstory species. A mixture of white ash, tupelo, and some scattered oaks also occur in the forested areas. A 2,144-acre tract within the National Natural Landmark Area was designated as a Wilderness Area. The American Bird Conservancy also has listed the refuge as a Globally Important Bird Area.

Cache River NWR was designated as a "Wetland of International Importance" in 1989, under the auspices of the "Convention on Wetlands of International Importance Especially as Waterfowl Habitat," commonly referred to as the Ramsar Convention. The Convention criteria, under which these lands qualified as the eighth U.S. Wetlands of International Importance, were: (1) Volume of use by migratory and resident waterfowl, especially mallards; (2) outstanding example of a wetland community characteristic of its bio-geographic region; (3) endangered species; (4) species diversity; (5) research value; and (6) practicality of conservation and management (AGFC 1989).

The Cache River Natural Area, dedicated by the Arkansas Natural Heritage Commission (ANHC) in 1982, is a 937-acre area located within the AGFC Rex Hancock/Black Swamp Wildlife Management Area, which is intermingled with tracts of the Cache River NWR. This Natural Area contains outstanding examples of cypress-tupelo swamp and willow-oak forest. Cypress trees in this and several other locations within the ecosystem are estimated to be in excess of 500-1,000 years old by University of Arkansas dendrochronological research (e.g., Stahle et al. 1985).

Wapanocca NWR was named as a Continentally Important Bird Area by the American Bird Conservancy because of its significant numbers of herons and waterfowl.

ECOSYSTEM CONTEXT

OVERVIEW

The Service is increasing its efforts, within the ecosystem management context, to adopt collaborative resource partnerships with private landowners and local communities, as well as state and federal governments. The purpose is to reduce the declining trend of fish and wildlife populations and biological diversity, to establish conservation priorities, to clarify goals, and to solve common threats and problems associated with fish and wildlife resources. The synergy of unified efforts of federal, state, tribal, and private organizations will ensure that the more important habitat areas are protected and that redundancy and overlap in conservation efforts are avoided.

The refuges within the Complex are members and active participants of the Service's Lower Mississippi River Ecosystem Team (Figure 2). The Lower Mississippi River Ecosystem (LMRE) is the primary wintering habitat for mid-continent waterfowl populations, as well as breeding and migrating habitat for songbirds returning from Central and South America, while providing high-quality habitat for resident wildlife species.

Geographically, the refuges lie on the northwestern boundary of the LMRE. The refuges have opportunities to contribute to many of the goals and objectives established for the protection and management of the LMRE.

LOWER MISSISSIPPI RIVER ECOSYSTEM PRIORITIES

Goals identified by the Lower Mississippi River Ecosystem Team to which the refuges can contribute include:

Goal 1. Conserve, enhance, protect, and monitor migratory bird populations and their habitats in the LMRE.

Goal 2. Protect, restore, and manage the wetlands of the LMRE.

Goal 3. Protect and/or restore imperiled habitats and viable populations of all threatened, endangered, and candidate species and species of concern in the LMRE.

Figure 2. Location of Central Arkansas NWR Complex in the LMRE

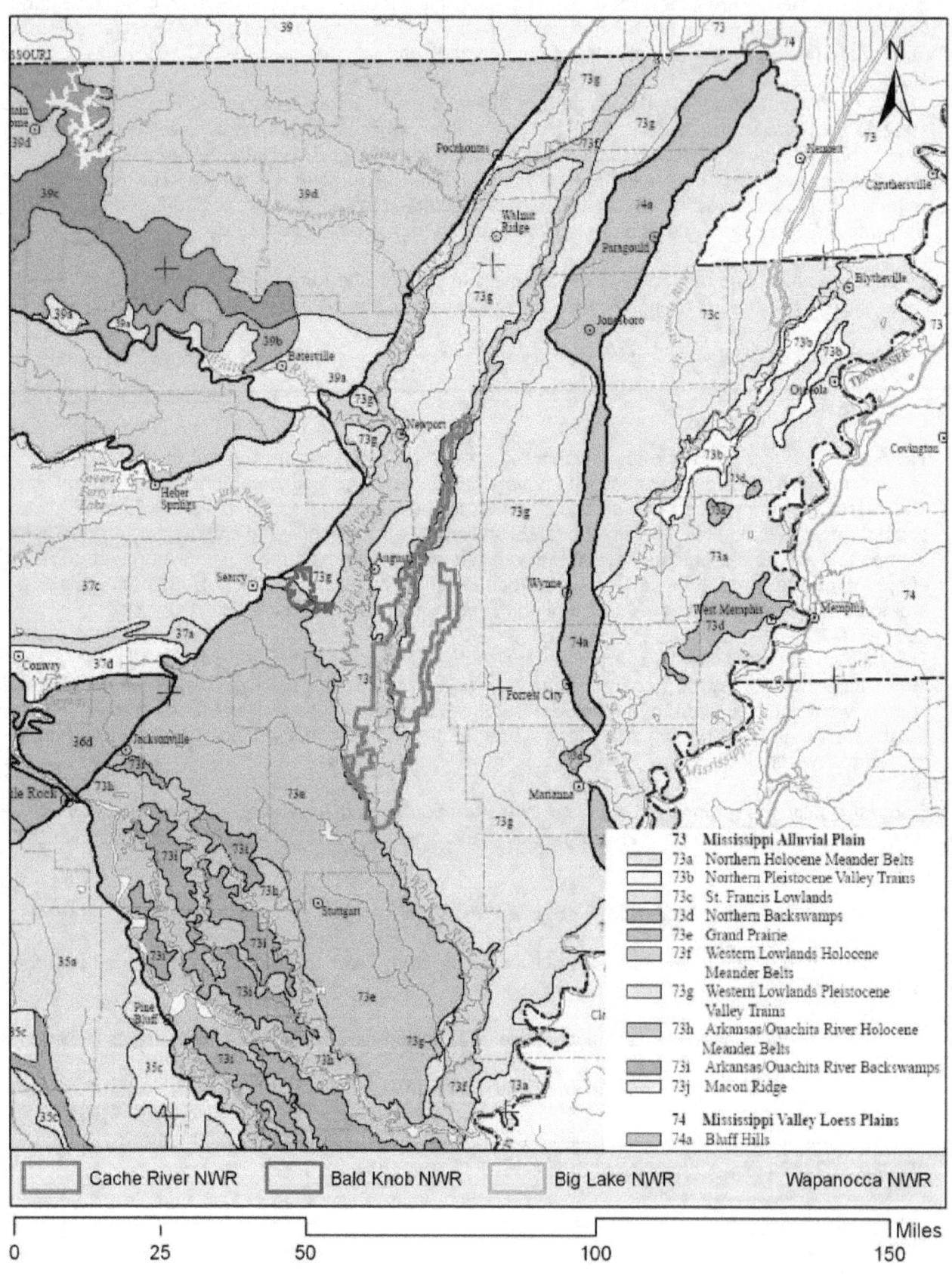

73   Mississippi Alluvial Plain
- 73a   Northern Holocene Meander Belts
- 73b   Northern Pleistocene Valley Trains
- 73c   St. Francis Lowlands
- 73d   Northern Backswamps
- 73e   Grand Prairie
- 73f   Western Lowlands Holocene Meander Belts
- 73g   Western Lowlands Pleistocene Valley Trains
- 73h   Arkansas/Ouachita River Holocene Meander Belts
- 73i   Arkansas/Ouachita River Backswamps
- 73j   Macon Ridge

74   Mississippi Valley Loess Plains
- 74a   Bluff Hills

Cache River NWR   Bald Knob NWR   Big Lake NWR   Wapanocca NWR

0   25   50   100   150   Miles

Goal 4. Protect, restore, and manage the fisheries and other aquatic resources historically associated with the wetlands and waters of the LMRE.

Goal 5. Restore, manage, and protect national wildlife refuges and national fish hatcheries.

Goal 6. Increase public awareness and support for LMRE resources and their management.

Goal 7. Enforce natural resource laws.

Goal 8. Protect, restore, and enhance water and air quality throughout the LMRE.

REGIONAL CONSERVATION PLANS AND INITIATIVES

THE BIG WOODS OF ARKANSAS

The Nature Conservancy (Conservancy or TNC) and its partners, including the Service, have protected more than 120,000 acres in the Big Woods of Arkansas, a 550,000-acre corridor of floodplain forest along the Mississippi River. Some of the corridor includes Refuge System lands. In 2004, the Ivory-billed Woodpecker, thought to be extinct, was re-discovered within the corridor. Major restoration and conservation priorities for the Big Woods have been identified. Efforts by the Conservancy, the Service, the ANHC, the AGFC, and others continue to focus on these ecologically important lands.

ARKANSAS WILDLIFE ACTION PLAN

Each state, including Arkansas, has developed a wildlife action plan to determine comprehensive wildlife conservation strategies for flora and fauna within the state. The plan identified 18 categories of threats to the wildlife of Arkansas, the condition of the state's wildlife health, and determined associated management actions needed to conserve wildlife and important habitat before they become more rare and costly to protect. Many of these threats are also of concern to the Service, such as hydrological alteration, habitat destruction, contaminants, predation and disease, and resource depletion. The Service and the AGFC work cooperatively on many projects to combat the effects of these threats.

ECOLOGICAL THREATS AND PROBLEMS

National wildlife refuges in the Lower Mississippi Valley (LMV) serve as part of the last safety net to support biological diversity, the greatest conservation challenge facing the Service. According to the LMRE Team, the greatest threats to biological diversity within the LMV are:

- the loss of sustainable natural communities, including the loss of 20 million acres of bottomland hardwood forests;

- the loss of connectivity between bottomland hardwood forest sites (e.g., forest fragmentation);

- the effects of agricultural and timber harvesting practices;

- the simplification of gene pools and the remaining wildlife habitats within the ecosystem;

- the effects of constructing navigation and water diversion projects; and

- the cumulative habitat effects of land and water resource development activities.

Specific threats applicable to Complex include:

- altered hydrology, stream flows, and flooding regimes, and reduced water quality;

- colonization of invasive plant and animal species, which displace natural vegetation and degrade those habitats on which native animal species depend;

- loss of freshwater source for Wapanocca Lake;

- deposition of sediment, trash, and pollutants resulting from flood events in the Missouri bootheel into Big Lake, and

- potential on-site impacts of off-site oil and gas development.

CLIMATE

The climate of central and eastern Arkansas can be characterized as mild and moderately humid. The mean monthly minimum temperature at Stuttgart is 39.7°F in January, and the mean monthly maximum is 91.1°F in July. Winters are relatively mild, but brief cold periods occur occasionally. The region has a long growing season, ranging from approximately 200 days in the north to 220 days in the south, and extended hot, humid periods are common during the summer, with maximum temperatures often exceeding 100°F during July and August.

The region receives abundant precipitation, ranging from 48 to 51 inches annually. Although rainfall is considered to be well distributed throughout the year (the average number of days with measurable precipitation is about 100 per year), there is a pronounced seasonal pattern. Almost one-third of the annual rainfall occurs during March, April, and May, with the driest months being July through October. The average annual evaporation is about 37 inches, with approximately 23 inches occurring from May through September, which exceeds the average rainfall during this period by about 5 inches. The average annual runoff throughout this region is 16 to 20 inches, most occurring from November through April (Friewald 1985). These climatic characteristics are important in driving the hydrology of the watershed, which is in turn the most critical component in shaping ecosystem functions and processes.

Geology and Topography

Geology and topography for the Cache River NWR is representative of all four refuges within the Central Arkansas NWR Complex. Specific details regarding Bald Knob, Big Lake, and Wapanocca NWRs can be requested from each refuge. The discussion below will give the reader a general sense of the geology and topography for all the refuges within the Complex.

An understanding of the basic geology of Arkansas' Delta is important for understanding the interrelationships of the soil and hydrologic components and processes of the ecosystem, which provide the basis for the associated biotic communities. Paleozoic bedrock outcrops occur on the western edge of the Delta, and declines to the southeast, where outcrops are overlain by more recent alluvial and loessal strata deposited during alternating inundations and recessions of the Gulf of Mexico. The bedrock below the Cache/Lower White Rivers' system originated nearly 1,000 to over 4,000 feet below sea level. Various overlying strata of gravel and sand support several important and productive aquifers, alternating with confining strata of silts and clays (ASWCC 1988).

The surface strata of the Cache/Lower White Rivers' basin are all Quaternary deposits of alluvium and loess. Holocene alluvial deposits of the existing major rivers, abandoned meanders, and areas near channels form the current "bottomland" areas. These are the lowest areas in the basin, and most likely to be forested and retain other obvious wetland characteristics. Immediately upslope of these most recent deposits are one or more terraces of Pleistocene alluvial deposits. Lands at this and higher elevations are the ones which have largely been cleared for agricultural production. Older deposits are exposed in only very limited circumstances in the basin. These include an area of dune sand located in Woodruff County between the Cache River and Bayou DeView, and some isolated pockets of exposed silt and sand along Bayou DeView north and east of Jonesboro.

The elevation at the north end of the basin at the Missouri state line is approximately 300' mean sea level (MSL), compared to 125' MSL at the mouth of the White River. This drop in elevation across 185 air miles represents an average slope of only 0.018 percent (approximately 1 ft/1 mi) across the entire basin. Although relatively flat, the topography of the basin can be somewhat complex, with numerous current stream and river channels, old meanders, and oxbow lakes surrounded by one or more terrace levels or bottoms.

The topography is usually one of three basic types: braided-stream terraces which display a characteristic dendritic drainage pattern; meander belts which contain areas of past or present channel migration with numerous parallel, crescent-shaped ridges and swales; and backswamps, which are flat areas that remained peripheral to channel migration and slowly filled with layers of fine sediments. Thus, in contrast to the apparent "flatness" of the landscape, the subtle complexity resulting from past and ongoing geologic forces has a dramatic and pronounced effect on the processes which drive this ecosystem and its functions. These processes in turn dictate the complexity of associated biologic communities that evolved here.

SOILS

A casual examination of any of the county soil surveys for the basin provides further visual reinforcement of the inherent complexity of the system. The majority of the soil types in the basin is hydric. The spatial relationships of the various soil types and associations present further evidence of their fluvial origin and influence. By and large, the soils of the basin are rich and fertile, and thus the reason for draining and clearing of most of the original forests for agricultural production. Most of the soils have a high clay content, which results in their capability to perch water at the surface, but this also prevents most areas from contributing to significant groundwater recharge through infiltration. These soil characteristics allow the cultivation of rice over a significant percentage of the lands in the basin. Where water retention and flooding characteristics of individual soils are not suited to rice, the dominant crops are soybeans, winter wheat, and milo, with minor acreages of corn and cotton occurring on the highest, most well-drained sites. Physiochemical and physiographic characteristics of soils (e.g., high clay content, susceptibility to erosion, water retention capabilities, and compressibility), and their relationships to ongoing hydrologic processes necessitate careful consideration during assessment of potential impacts of management and land use activities, if restoration and conservation of ecosystem functions are to be successful.

HYDROLOGY

Bald Knob and Cache River NWRs

A basic appreciation of the hydrology of the Cache/Lower White Rivers' ecosystem, and recognition and acknowledgement of its importance as the driving force behind all other ecosystem processes and functions is fundamental to addressing long-term conservation. Without this explicit recognition by all partners, effective long-term management of public lands within the basin is impossible, and efforts toward meaningful, sustainable restoration of ecosystem functions cannot be effective or adequately focused. Although a thorough understanding and comparison of the past and present hydrologic function of the system would be desirable, available data are inadequate. However, the basic concepts and generalizations which are known can contribute significantly to providing context and direction to management of the public lands within the ecosystem, and to addressing the influence of the surrounding agricultural landscape.

Pre-settlement Conditions – The Cache/Lower White Rivers' ecosystem was a forested wetland habitat complex whose composition, structure, and function were largely determined by the frequency, duration, and depth of inundation. The Cache River drainage area is 1,037 mi² and that of Bayou DeView is 421 mi². The abundant annual rainfall, flat topographic profile, and other hydrologic influences resulted in flooding, which ranged from frequent, deep, and prolonged events adjacent to the major drainages and in the lower portion of the system, to shallow and temporary events in the topographically higher areas of the bottoms and in isolated, but often extensive depressions throughout the terrace lands. The annual hydrologic cycle reflected seasonal rainfall patterns, with lowest flows occurring in July through October, and flooding along the river bottoms typically beginning in December or January and peaking in February and March on the Cache River and Bayou DeView and in April and May on the lower White River (ASWCC 1988). The system contained an abundance of stream channels, sloughs, oxbow lakes, and scrub-shrub swamps, which contained water throughout the year in all but the driest years. Extremely dry periods, during which a significant percentage of the smaller stream channels (on the order of Cache River and smaller) were exposed, were infrequent but must have occurred every few hundred years as evidenced by (1) the current distribution of bald cypress, which can survive but not germinate in inundated circumstances, and (2) documentation through a 400+ year-flow reconstruction based on a dendrochronological study of old-growth bald cypress trees on the Cache River (Cleaveland et al. 1988). The extreme dynamism of the hydrology within the system, over both the short- and long-term, was one of its most important pre-settlement characteristics.

There also was and is a significant degree of spatial variation in the hydrology within the ecosystem. Relatively shallow depressions in the bottomlands and terraces are the first areas to be annually influenced by inundation through a process termed "puddling," when they gradually fill during the onset of fall rains in November. With continuing rainfall, these areas expand and interconnect, affecting larger and larger acreages. These depressions would also have been among the last seasonally inundated wetlands to dry during late spring with the end of the rainy period. With the continuation of fall rains, the upper reaches of the streams' floodplains were largely affected by "headwater flooding," the relatively rapid flooding of drainage areas due to heavy rainfalls during short periods of time. Heavy rains, in conjunction with the natural constraints of small channels and broad, vegetated floodplains, can exceed the short-term capacity of the system to carry away the rainfall. As this process proceeded with additional winter and spring rains, gradually pushing major drainages like the White and Mississippi Rivers to capacity, larger areas of flats and floodplains were inundated by "backwater flooding." This was caused by water "backing" into higher areas as a result of flows greatly in excess of stream channel capacities and/or impeded drainage in lower portions of the system. For example, high flows on the Mississippi River greatly affect the hydrology of the lower half of the White River NWR by reducing the ability of the White River to discharge into it; conversely, high flows of the White River may be relatively easily carried if the Mississippi River is low. The same situation exists at the confluence of the Cache and White Rivers at Clarendon, and at other tributary confluences on a smaller scale. Thus, there were complex hydrologic interrelationships between the tributaries and primary rivers within the ecosystem, including the lower White River and Arkansas and Mississippi Rivers.

Hydrologic Modifications – Unfortunately, these hydrologic patterns and relationships and their effects on other functions of the Cache/Lower White Rivers' basin have often been inadequately considered as it has been incrementally but significantly altered since settlement. It is helpful to view the hydrologic alteration of the Cache/Lower White Rivers within the perspective of historic flood control and drainage policies of the MAV as a whole (Baxter and Sunderland 1985). During settlement in the late 1800s and early 1900s, there were many uncoordinated, local flood control and drainage projects. Although these early projects may have had a significant cumulative impact on the terrace lands within the ecosystem, they had less effect on natural headwater and backwater flooding of the major drainages. However, subsequent to the major Mississippi River flood of 1927, when much of the Arkansas Delta was inundated, a comprehensive federal flood control program was initiated. This resulted in the construction of the mainstem Mississippi River levees, and levee projects on major tributaries such as the White River. These projects constricted the floodplains of the Mississippi River and its tributaries such that lower flows now result in higher elevations of flooding than was the case for pre-settlement hydrology. Additionally, headwater dams at Greers Ferry, Bull Shoals, and Norfork were installed as part of the comprehensive federal response to the 1927 floods. Operation of these dams have affected downstream peak flood flows and lowered summer/fall base flows.

One of the by-products of the subsequent era of major flood control projects was the extensive conversion of bottomland hardwoods to agricultural production, much of it occurring in the Cache/Lower White Rivers' basin during the 1940s through the mid-1970s. Land that was provided protection from flooding by these major levee systems was quickly cleared and brought into agricultural production. Extensive conversion of bottomland hardwood forests to agricultural lands has negatively impacted the hydrological regime of the Cache/Lower White Rivers' basin, as well as the Lower Mississippi Alluvial Valley as a whole. The clearing of forest, increased the "flashiness" of streams due to accelerated run off, and exacerbated siltation in streams and wetland systems due to increased sediment transport. The federal Flood Control Acts of 1944 and 1965 promoted a policy of bottomland hardwood conversion, and the 1965 Act included as a part of its justification the clearing of 4.9 million acres in the MAV (Baxter and Sunderland 1985), much ultimately occurring in the Cache/Lower White River basin. With this federal policy in place, many local drainage/flood control projects, now coordinated to some extent by the U.S. Army Corps of Engineers (COE or Corps), continued up the tributaries through the mid-1980s. Beginning in the early 1900s and continuing until the early 1930s, local drainage districts channelized the upper portion of the Cache River basin, from Grubbs (river mile 128 of 203), at the north end of the Cache River NWR acquisition boundary, to its headwaters. The lower seven miles of the Cache River were also channelized in the early 1970s, but this project was stopped by legal action, and the overall hydrologic impacts of this 7-mile modification are unquantified.

The collective results of over a century of flood control activities has been (1) the draining and clearing of the vast majority of the terrace lands and driest portions of the forested wetland habitats of the entire system, especially within the Cache River/Bayou DeView basin where clearing to the riverbanks has occurred in many areas; (2) constriction of the floodplain of the Lower White River with levees, and the clearing of lands protected by those levees; and (3) the modification of the natural hydrologic patterns (e.g., timing, frequency, and flow rates) throughout the ecosystem. It should be noted that from the biological perspective, these alterations have occurred within a single generation of trees, which constitutes a significant biological alteration. Approximately 85 percent of the basin has been cleared of its hardwoods, and most of these lands were forested wetlands.

A relatively recent and continuing hydrologic modification is the increasing withdrawal of surface water from essentially all available streams for agricultural irrigation. These withdrawals occur at the farm level, are individually relatively small, but are cumulative in their effect throughout the basin. There is no available estimate of current withdrawal rates, but they are known to be collectively substantial. For example, portions of the Cache River, with a relatively low base flow, are frequently pumped dry for some periods during most summers. Similarly, the upper portion of Bayou DeView usually has no base flow during some summer months, and agricultural pumping has exacerbated this to the point that the stream has recorded no-flow conditions for 10 percent of the time over the last 37 years and has been designated as a "critical surface water area" by the State of Arkansas (ASWCC 1988). However, in contradiction to the previously described long-term effects of flood control and regulation projects, the recent average streamflow of the White River at Clarendon has decreased slightly, and this has been speculated to be the result of current withdrawals for irrigation. Several large-scale irrigation projects, including the Grand Prairie Area Demonstration Project, are being aggressively pursued by the Arkansas Natural Resources Commission, National Resources Conservation Service (NRCS), and Corps, with the White River being the primary source of irrigation.

Current Hydrologic Status – Even though the basic processes of puddling and headwater and backwater flooding still operate within the basin, their collective contribution to hydrologic function has been profoundly modified by both quantitative and qualitative alteration, and by the addition processes such as irrigation withdrawals. Interestingly, the overall hydrologic effects on the system can be described as being at both ends of the spectrum: drier in most areas, wetter in some. The many local efforts directed at drainage associated with agricultural production and transportation (e.g., road ditches) have significantly reduced the area affected by puddling and the amount of water that could be held as a result of puddling. Areas that were cleared of forest and ditched now contribute virtually none of their original hydrologic function to the system by immediately discharging excess rainfall as runoff to the watercourses. When the acreage that has been influenced by flood control projects intended to reduce the impacts of headwater flooding are added to these, then the vast majority of the ecosystem is now affected. This area no longer holds temporary water as it did historically, and now relatively rapidly discharges runoff to the rivers; thus, these areas, comprising most of the higher elevations of the ecosystem, are drier than they were historically, being inundated much less frequently and for much shorter durations.

However, as a direct result of the increased rate of drainage from most of the basin, the lower elevations and those areas nearest the Cache River, Bayou DeView, and White River now receive all this water more rapidly and in quantities more frequently exceeding the capacity of the system to carry and discharge into the Mississippi River. Additionally, the discharge capacity of the White River into the Mississippi River and Cache River into the White River is greatly reduced from historic conditions due to the effects of the levee projects. Thus, the areas immediately adjoining the upper and middle Cache River and Bayou DeView, subjected to unregulated flows, can be characterized as being more frequently flooded at greater depths, but for shorter durations than in the natural ecosystem. The stochastic dynamics of the natural system have in many ways been exaggerated by the hydrologic modifications. On the other hand, the lowest portions of the Cache and Lower White Rivers seem now to be subjected to more frequent flooding, at greater depths, for longer durations than was the historic tendency.

Big Lake NWR

An extensive network of ditches in the Missouri bootheel drains approximately 2,500 square miles directly through Big Lake NWR. The refuge is situated between Ditch 81 and its associated levee to the west and Ditch 28 and its levee to the east.

A Water Management Plan for the refuge establishes operating procedures set forth by the Corps (Memphis District). A 1989 agreement between the Corps and the Service addresses seasonal water level management. Refuge personnel operate five water control structures located in Ditch 81 and Ditch 28 in accordance with guidelines set forth in a Standing Instructions Manual, dated December 1991.

During flood periods the inflows are so heavily laden with silt that an accurate description of the water would be "too thick to drink and too thin to plow." Sediment fallout has provided continual fill to the bottomlands and swamp until there now exists a very shallow lake, averaging only 3 feet in depth. Continued siltation has restricted any aquatic production, and hampered forest growth and development. Under the Water Management Plan, the refuge has served primarily as a sump.

Approximately 15 miles of meandering stream channels run the length of the refuge, but past siltation has made portions of these channels indistinguishable. These channels were once a part of the Little River, but today only a small portion of the original river channel exists just south of the refuge.

Through mutual agreements with regional drainage districts, the Corps, the Service and local interest groups, a plan to improve the situation was implemented to divert some of the silt-laden waters around Big Lake and still provide for adequate inflow to maintain and hopefully improve the area's ecosystem.

Since the implementation of the new regime of water management, water quality has improved, aquatic production has returned, waterfowl populations have become more stable, threatened and endangered species have returned to the area, and recreational interests have increased. Additional water management practices are being explored, which should enhance the refuge's contribution toward the improvements even more.

Despite these improvements, the refuge is still frequently subjected to silt-laden flood waters due to continued drainage projects occurring upstream in Missouri. The frequency of the floods coupled with the silt and drift imported by floods are damaging to the refuge. Geologists from the University of Arkansas took core samples from the bottom of Big Lake in May 1991. Preliminary data from radiocarbon dating revealed that since 1938, more than 3 feet of silt have been deposited into Big Lake. Such siltation rates have greatly accelerated the eutrophication of the Big Lake system.

As long as Big Lake is subjected to the floods from the vast Missouri bootheel agricultural lands, the lake will continue to be filled with Missouri topsoil. Local fishermen complain of lower water levels and aquatic vegetation (e.g., lotus) where none was present 20 years ago. The 2,500-square-mile watershed from the Missouri bootheel provided adequate water supplies during the year. The water was delivered to the head of Big Lake by way of four major drainage ditches. As long as incoming flows were less than 238' msl, refuge personnel manipulated water control structures to create inflows of good quality water into the refuge or to divert poor quality (e.g., muddy) water around the refuge via the diversion canal. When water levels exceeded 238' msl, the refuge operated both the Diversion and North-end structures in the open position to aid in the movement and storage of flood waters as directed in a multi-agency water management agreement.

To provide water to the Hornersville Swamp Conservation Area (CA) and the Big Lake Wildlife Management Area during waterfowl hunting seasons, the Diversion Channel and North-end structures are operated in a manual mode. As directed in the water management plan, the following elevations immediately upstream of the structure are to be maintained during the specified times:

- Maintain an elevation not to exceed 235.5 National Geodetic Vertical Datum (NGVD) (plus or minus 0.5) from September 15 through October 14.

- Maintain an elevation not to exceed 236.5 NGVD (plus or minus 0.5) from October 15 through October 31.

- Maintain an elevation not to exceed 239.0 NGVD from November 1 through November 15.

- Maintain an elevation not to exceed 236.5 NGVD (plus or minus 0.5) for the remainder of the Arkansas and Missouri winter waterfowl hunting seasons.

When the area receives average fall and winter precipitation, the refuge structures can be operated to easily provide these water levels that will in turn flood the Big Lake WMA to target water levels. The Hornersville Swamp CA will have sufficient water for waterfowl hunting when the level is near 239'msl. As a general rule for every inch of rain that falls across the bootheel of Missouri, a foot rise in water at the North-end can be expected within 24 hours. Under flood conditions that generally follow several consecutive rain events, it can be impossible to maintain levels under 238' msl even with all Diversion and North-end gates fully open. During waterfowl hunting season in the Hornersville Swamp CA and Big Lake WMA, flooding is usually welcomed as these conditions allow boat access to more areas. With the Big Lake WMA's levee degraded to 237.4'msl in several areas, these high water events are an unwelcome site during the summer growing seasons.

Wapanocca NWR

Wapanocca Lake is an oxbow that was formed when the main channel of the Mississippi River changed its course. Historically, Mississippi River flood events would periodically refresh Wapanocca Lake, but this hydrologic regime was permanently eliminated by the construction of the Mississippi River levee by the Corps, 2.5 miles east of the current refuge boundary. Currently, the only source of water to the lake is from the small watershed between the refuge and the Mississippi River levee. During extreme rain events, ephemeral streams and ditches within the watershed will carry water to Ditch 8, which enters on the east side of the refuge, and can then be diverted into the east end of Woody Pond and eventually into the east end of Wapanocca Lake. However, this process is inadequate to provide a sufficient and timely water source to the lake. Opportunities to input water from Ditch 12 on the North end of Wapanocca Lake are much more frequent, but due to findings of heavy metals within Ditch 12, it is no longer allowed.

Seven drainage ditches (numbers 1, 2, 3, 4, 5, 8, and 13) flow through the refuge. An eighth, number 12, connects with Big Creek and the middle of this ditch is the north boundary of the refuge.

WATER QUALITY AND QUANTITY

Historical data on water quality parameters for the refuges are largely absent. Water quality in pre-settlement times, as in most areas, would be expected to have been good. Water throughout this extensive wetland system, with little erosion except for bank erosion along rivers, would have been anticipated to be relatively clear. In fact, some current long-time residents at the Cache River describe it as being clear as recently as 50 years ago. However, it is apparent that the byproducts of land clearing and subsequent agricultural production on most of the basin's surface area are now driving water quality parameters. The U.S. Geological Survey (1984) cited potential pollution of groundwater and accumulation of pesticides in bottom sediments as a major concern, although it indicated that potential effects were not quantified in eastern Arkansas.

Due to recent (since approximately 1975) water quality monitoring programs of agencies such as Environmental Protection Agency (EPA), U.S. Geological Survey (USGS), and the Arkansas Department of Environmental Quality (ADEQ), there is currently a relative abundance of data (approximately 13 monitoring stations) for the Cache/Lower White Rivers' ecosystem. A USGS trends analysis (Petersen 1990) provides some summary information on some aspects of current water quality trends in the basin in relation to other areas in eastern Arkansas. Typical values of total recoverable manganese and total 2,4-D are higher in the Cache River than any other river group in the region; dieldrin concentrations are highest here along with the St. Francis River; total phosphorus, biochemical oxygen demand, and fecal-coliform bacteria values are generally higher than most other river groups; and, specific conductance, total alkalinity, and total hardness values are lower than other groups except Bayou Meto. In general, these factors are indicative of a wetland system significantly impacted by agriculture. A 2001 study by North Carolina State University, "Chemical Contamination at National Wildlife Refuges in the Lower Mississippi River Ecosystem," identified some evidence of contaminant hazard associated with organochlorine pesticides and current use pesticides.

Most of the water quality problems of the system are associated directly or indirectly with erosion of sediment from agricultural lands into the streams. Many of the chemical constituents mentioned above are bound to and carried by sediment particles. Turbidity values for Cache River/Bayou DeView were accordingly higher than any other river group in eastern Arkansas (Petersen 1988). Petersen (1988) documented annual suspended sediment discharges at the Patterson and Cotton Plant stations to be 96,800 and 78,500 tons, respectively, in 1987; however, these discharges were not normally distributed over time, with 22 percent of the annual sediment discharge occurring during a 10-day flood event in mid-winter. A study on the Cache River at AGFC Rex Hancock/Black Swamp WMA documented sedimentation accretion rates of up to 2.5 cm/year (Kleiss 1996). In this case, approximately 30 miles of Cache River wetlands were responsible for decreasing the suspended sediment load by an annual average (3 years of data) of 14 percent. However, although sediment retention is a natural function of forested wetlands, this rate of removal of sediment is unnatural and unsustainable over time if maintenance or restoration of wetland functions and values is desirable. This point is supported by dendrogeomorphic analyses, which indicated that historic sedimentation rates in the area may have been as low as 0.01 cm/yr, but that rates increased sharply from less than 0.13 cm/yr immediately prior to 1945 to a mean rate of 0.29 cm/yr from 1981-90 (Hupp and Morris 1990). This significant increase, 30-times greater than estimated natural rates, corresponded with accelerated clearing of forested acreage for agriculture.

BIOLOGICAL RESOURCES

HABITAT

Bald Knob and Cache River NWRs are located within close proximity to one another and have similar habitats. Major forest habitat types for Bald Knob and Cacher River NWRs are depicted in Figures 3 and 5 (a and b), respectively.

Bald Knob NWR

Habitat/land use types represented on Bald Knob NWR are as follows:

Cropland	4,393 acres
Reforestation	6,188 acres
Bottomland hardwood forest	3,969 acres
Sloughs, ditches and other water	232 acres
Administrative lands	184 acres
Old fields	56 acres

Bounded on the south and east by the Little Red River and characterized by Overflow Creek, which winds through its middle, Bald Knob NWR contains a mixture of cypress-tupelo brakes, oxbow lakes, bottomland hardwoods, recently reforested lands, moist-soil impoundments, and agricultural fields. This variety of habitats supports a tremendous array of plants and animals, particularly migratory birds, throughout the year.

Figure 3. Forest Types on Bald Knob NWR

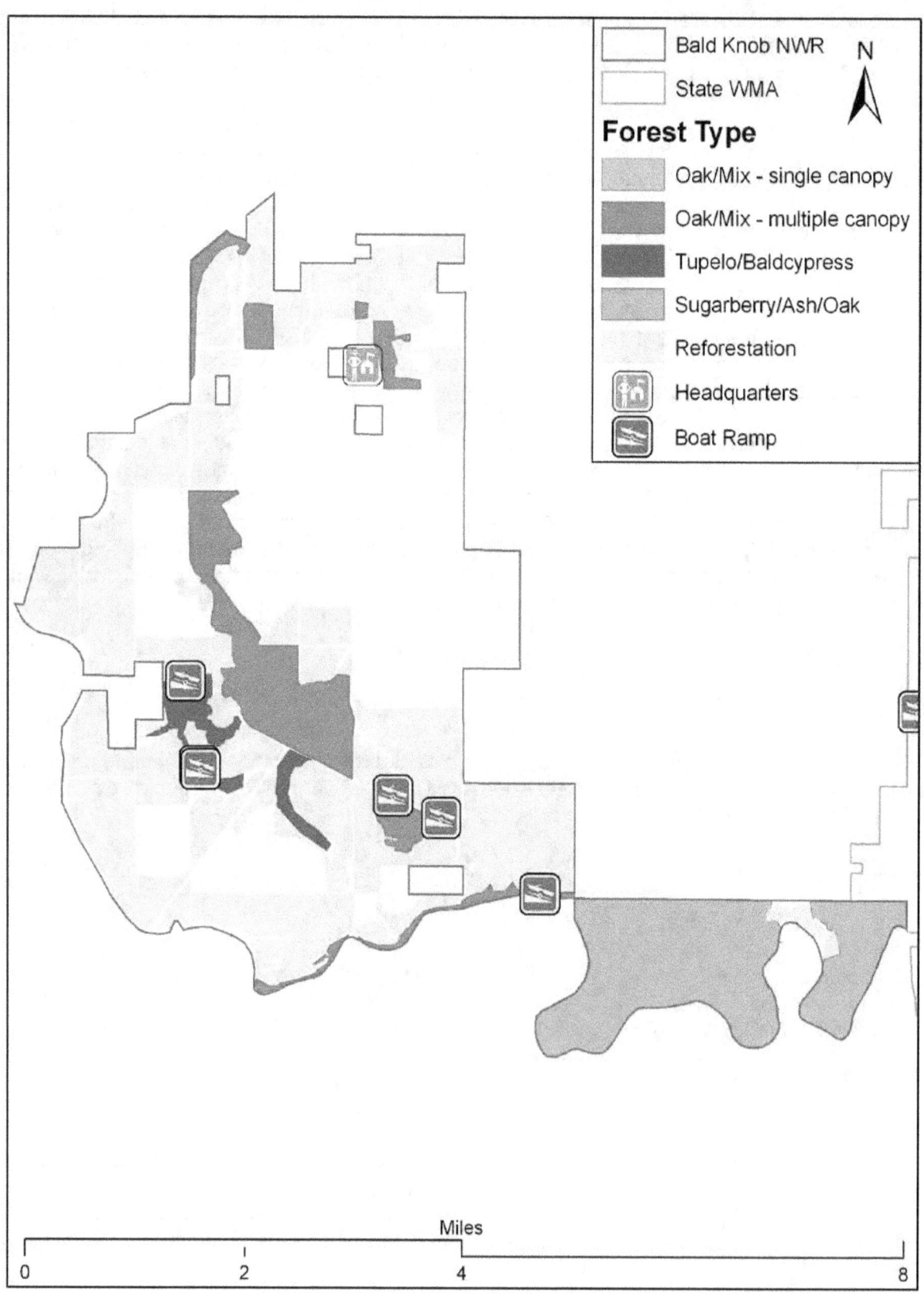

Central Arkansas National Wildlife Refuge Complex

There are now over 16 miles of refuge boundary along the Little Red River. The Mingo Creek Unit lies 3 miles west of the confluence of the Little Red River and the White River. These rivers are key water sources for the refuge, which depends on backwater flooding from the White River, which in turn causes the Little Red River to flood. Precise water management is obtained by cooperative pumping and maintenance agreements within the cooperative farming contract. All water utilized on the refuge is pumped from the Little Red River and is subsequently delivered to individual fields by gravity flow or re-lift pumping.

The refuge was staffed with a manager in 1997 and an engineering equipment operator in 1998. At that time, wildlife management focused on the primary purpose for refuge establishment, which is "conservation of winter habitat for key groups of waterfowl." Management actions involved cooperative farming to provide high energy foods such as rice, milo, and millet for migratory birds via flooding of crops, canal/levee maintenance, creating moist-soil units, repair/construction of water control structures, restoration of bottomland hardwood forests, and initiating compatible public hunt programs.

The recommendation from the 1998 Biological Review to reforest several thousand acres on Bald Knob NWR to provide a corridor that connects the Hurricane Wildlife Management Area and the refuge to the Ozark foothills has been accomplished, and reforestation likely will continue on future inholding purchases. Native oaks, cypress, sweetgum, pecan, and other hardwood species planted in former agricultural fields will greatly enhance habitat diversity for wildlife. In addition, scrub-shrub habitat has increased due to the amount of reforestation that has occurred over the past 10 years. Although the extent of agricultural crops has been reduced from over 10,000 acres in 1995 to 4,393 acres currently, the production of cereal grains, such as rice and milo, continues to provide a critically important food resource for wintering waterfowl. In addition, approximately 1,600 acres of moist-soil impoundments provide seeds and invertebrates for waterfowl, shorebirds, wading birds, and other wetland-dependent wildlife species.

The most unique feature of Bald Knob NWR is the water control infrastructure system available to precisely manage water quantity and depth. Nearly 80 miles of ditches and canals exist and are necessary to effectively drain, irrigate, and flood agricultural and moist-soil habitats to create important wildlife habitat.

Big Lake NWR

Habitat/land use types represented on Big Lake NWR (Figure 4) are as follows:

Cropland	42 acres
Moist-soil units	250 acres
Marsh	300 acres
Forest	2,159 acres
Open water	2,600 acres
Swamp	5,250 acres
Levees/dikes/administrative area	437 acres

In the northern Arkansas/Missouri Bootheel region, the Big Lake area is the last remnant of what had been the vast Mississippi Delta forest. The fertile soils, which were once covered with bottomland hardwoods, are now row-cropped to produce soybeans and cotton. The refuge persists as a forested oasis in an agricultural desert, and this isolated area of natural beauty is cherished by citizens of Arkansas. Except for the spoil levees and administrative areas, the rest of the refuge is classified as wetlands. The land contour ranges from 223' msl in the deepest channels near the south end to 240' msl near the north end.

Figure 4. Habitat Types on Big Lake NWR

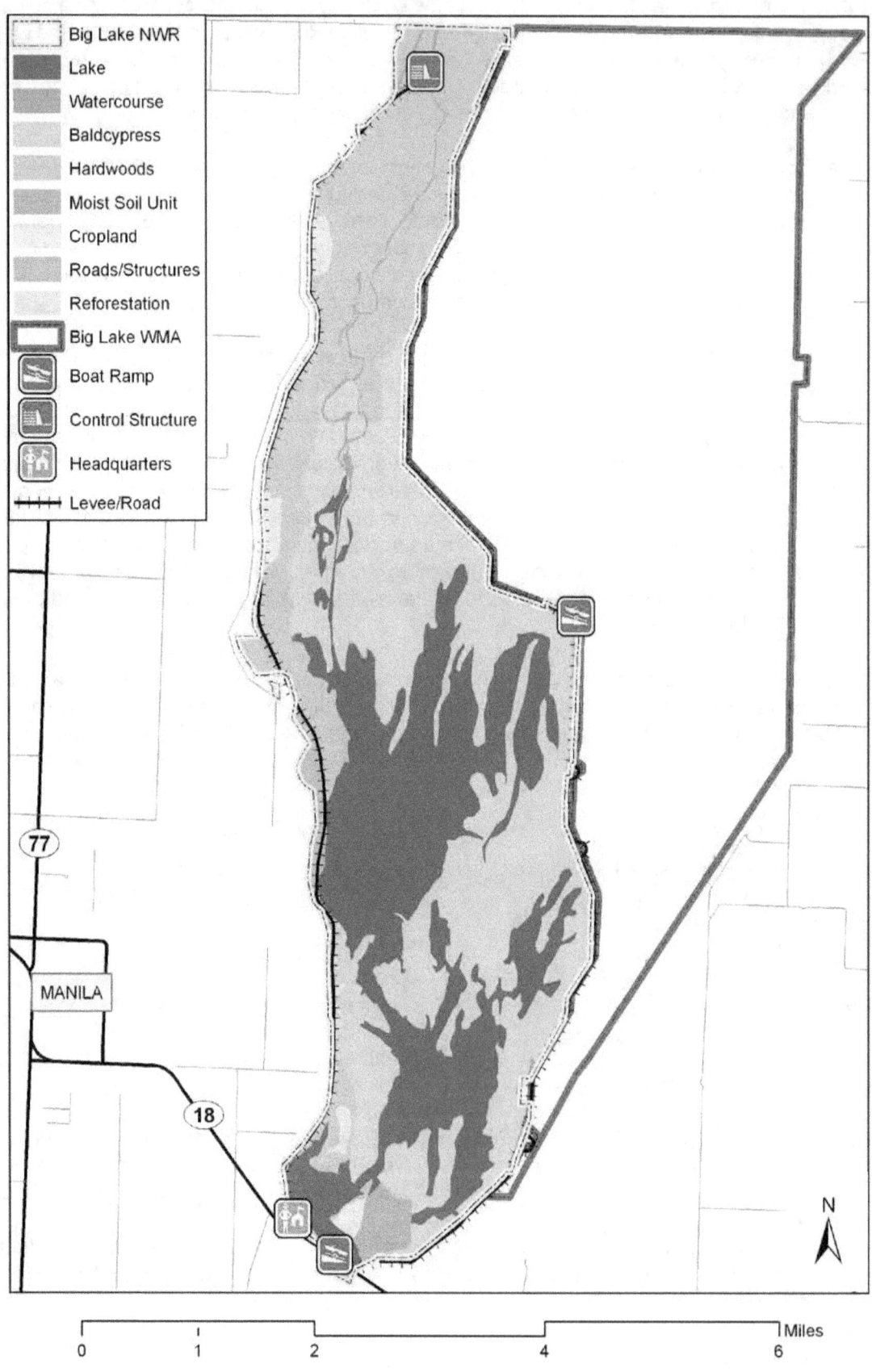

Cache River NWR

Habitat/land use types represented on Cache River NWR (Figures 5a and 5b) are as follows:

Cropland	3,106 acres
Moist-soil units	447 acres
Marsh	124 acres
Reforestation	15,524 acres
Bottomland hardwood forest	44,358 acres
Oxbow lakes, bayous, rivers	1,010 acres

Cache River NWR has utilized cooperative farming as one of several waterfowl management tools to meet waterfowl habitat objectives since the refuge's establishment in 1986. Rice, milo, soybeans, Japanese millet, and occasionally corn are grown on a rotating basis on the Dixie and Plunkett Farm Units. It should be noted that these two farm units are also used to meet refuge objectives for moist-soil plant production, winter browse, and migrating shorebird habitat in addition to row crop objectives for the refuge.

Despite the extensive and drastic drainage and channel alterations, the Cache River basin contains a variety of wetland communities, including some of the most intact and least disturbed bottomland hardwood forests in the Mississippi Valley region. These unique and valuable wetlands have been designated by the Ramsar Convention as "Wetlands of International Importance."

Forested land on Cache River NWR consists mostly of floodplain bottomland hardwoods, dominated by species such as willow oak, Nuttall oak, overcup oak, sugarberry, sweetgum, sweet pecan, bitter pecan, honey locust, persimmon, cypress, green ash, American elm, cedar elm, black willow, and red maple. Baldcypress-water tupelo swamps also comprise a significant portion of the lowest sites on the refuge.

During the last 15 or so years, more than 15,000 acres of agricultural and fallow fields have been planted in hardwood seedlings in an effort to link fragmented forested tracts and to create larger forest blocks for wildlife. Species planted include Nuttall oak, cherrybark oak, willow oak, water oak, overcup oak, sweet pecan, bald cypress, and a host of native hardwoods. Additional wetland areas on the refuge consist of approximately 447 acres of moist-soil units scattered throughout the farm fields. Moist-soil plants vary depending on the timing of drawdowns and soil disturbance, but usually consist of panic grass, smartweeds, sprangletop, millets, and a variety of sedges. An extensive network of lakes, streams, and bayous on the refuge provide an abundance of habitat for fishes, mussels, and other wetland-dependent species.

Wapanocca NWR

Habitat/land use types represented on Wapanocca NWR (Figure 6) are as follows:

Cropland	761	acres
Grassland	73	acres
Open water	612	acres
Swamp	1,760	acres
Moist-soil	288	acres
Reforestation	917	acres
Bottomland hardwood forest	1,502	acres

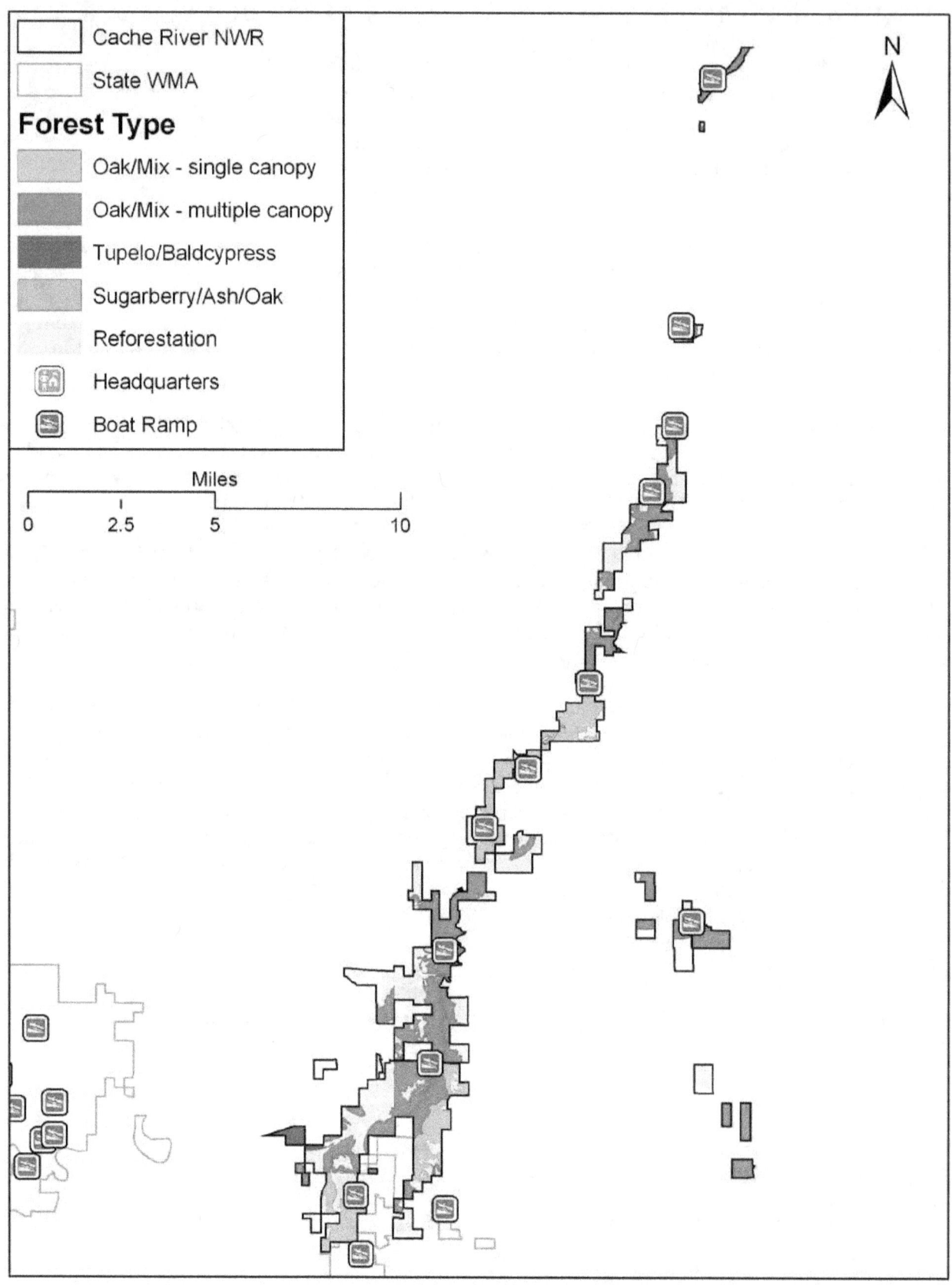

Figure 5b. Forest Types on Cache River NWR (South)

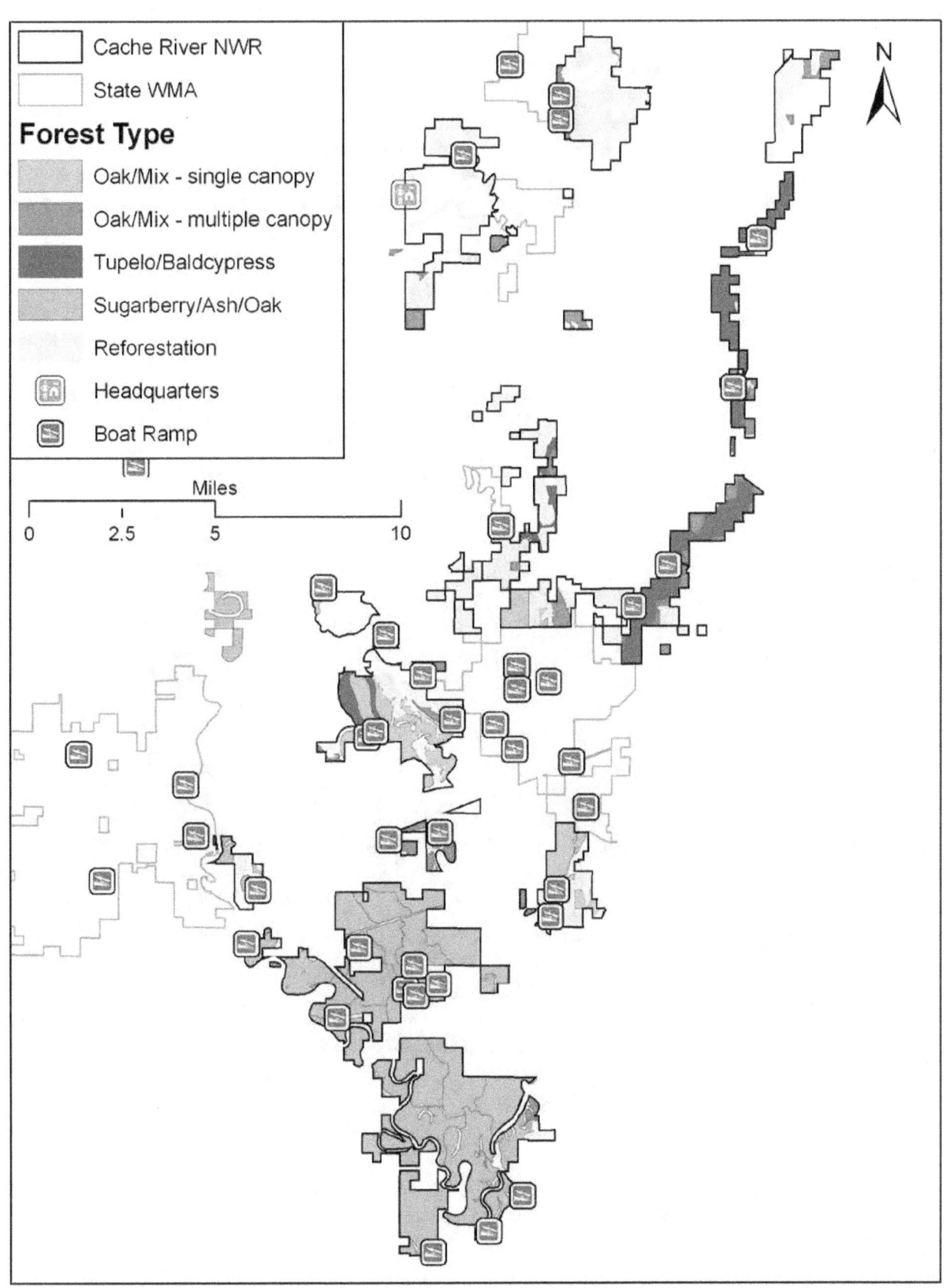

Legend:
- Cache River NWR
- State WMA

Forest Type
- Oak/Mix - single canopy
- Oak/Mix - multiple canopy
- Tupelo/Baldcypress
- Sugarberry/Ash/Oak
- Reforestation
- Headquarters
- Boat Ramp

Miles
0   2.5   5   10

Figure 6. Habitat types on Wapanocca NWR

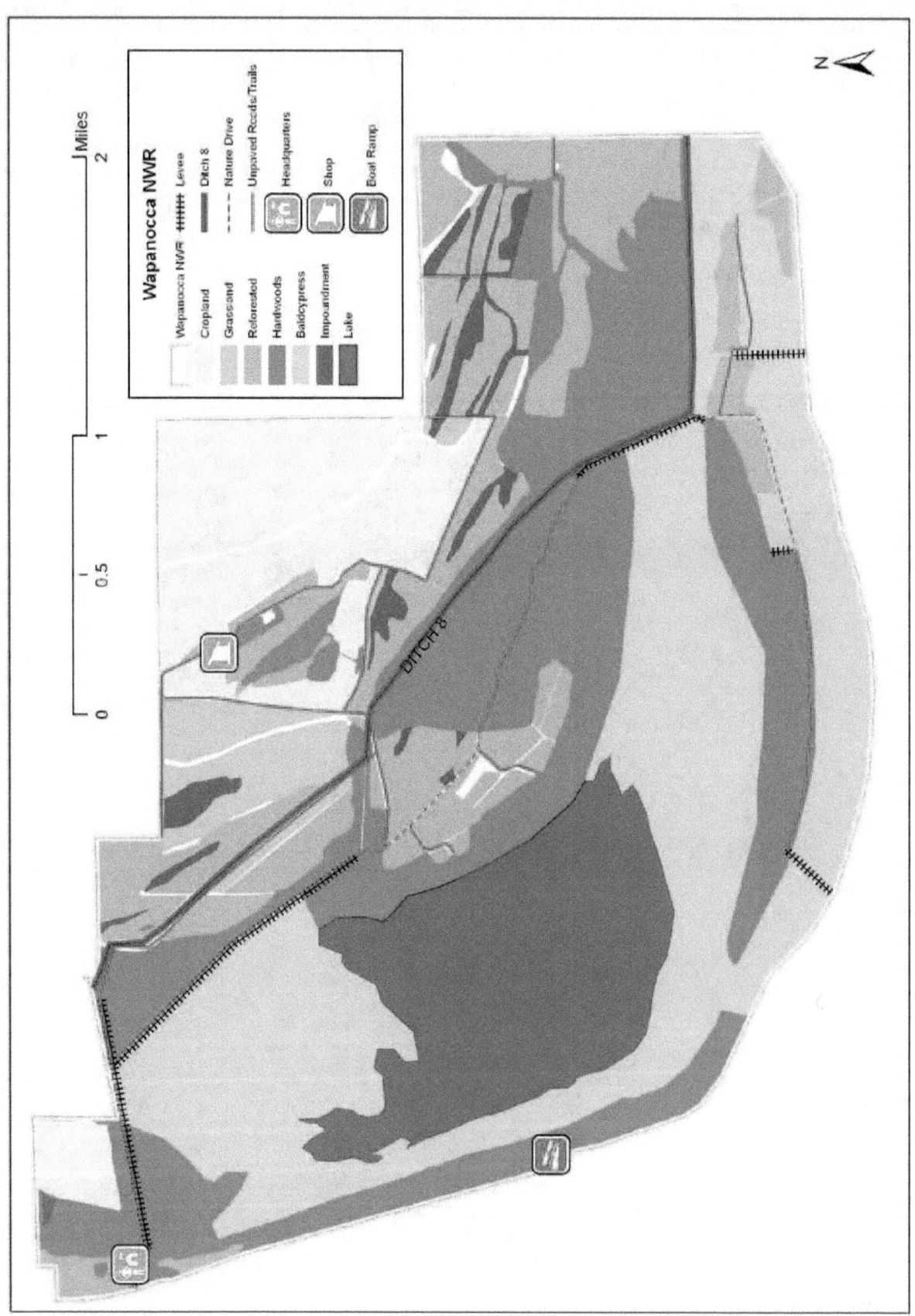

There is little old growth timber found on the refuge because it was logged while in private ownership. The invasive species Chinese privet and Japanese honeysuckle are common in the forested areas.

There are 32 small impoundments, with a total acreage of 288 acres with stoplog half-risers for water control. These impoundments are managed as moist-soil habitats for waterfowl, shorebirds, wading birds, and other native wildlife.

The Wapanocca Lake basin consists of 612 acres of open water and 1,200 acres of cypress/willow swamp. A concrete structure with two stoplog bays to control water levels is located at the northwest corner of the basin and empties into Big Creek. Woody Ponds is a 243-acre cypress swamp where water levels also are controlled by a stoplog structure. The remaining 317 acres of cypress swamps receive water from winter/spring flooding from ditch overflows and normally dry up during summer months.

WILDLIFE

Wildlife species that are known or expected to occur on the Central Arkansas NWR Complex are listed in Appendix G. Birds of conservation concern for the Mississippi Alluvial Valley (Bird Conservation Region 26) are listed by the refuge on which they occur in Appendix H. A brief discussion of wildlife species follows by refuge.

Bald Knob NWR

<u>Birds</u>

The refuge is noted for large numbers of wintering waterfowl, which have at times exceeded 650,000 birds. Mallards are the most numerous species, with Northern Pintail, American Wigeons, Gadwalls, Northern Shovelers, Green-winged and Blue-winged Teals, Scaup, Ring-necked Ducks, and Wood Ducks being common. The native Wood Duck and Hooded Merganser nest throughout the refuge. The refuge lies in the heart of the largest pintail wintering area in the state. As many as 250,000 pintail have been recorded wintering on the refuge. Peak waterfowl use normally occurs from November-December.

The refuge actively manages water and associated mudflats on approximately 150 acres for shorebirds. Shorebird use peaks around August 18, with approximately 5,000 birds. The most common species are Pectoral Sandpipers, Killdeer, Lesser Yellowlegs, Semi-palmated Plovers, Least Sandpipers, and Long-billed Dowitchers.

Marsh birds of primary concern in North America include King, Clapper, Virginia, Yellow, and Black Rails; Soras; American and Least Bitterns; Pied-billed Grebe; Purple Gallinule; and Common Moorhen. The refuge provides thousands of acres of suitable habitat for these migratory birds in any given year. While no confirmed nests have been recorded of any rail species, refuge personnel did observe a King Rail during June 2006. The American Bittern and Pied-billed Grebe are very common during spring migration, while the Least Bittern has been less documented. The only sighting of a Common Moorhen occurred during late spring 2007 by refuge personnel.

American, Common and Snowy Egrets; Great Blue and Little Blue Herons; and a host of other marsh birds utilize the various wetlands on the refuge throughout the year. Apart from the Great Blue Heron, which is a year-long resident, the other species usually arrive on the refuge around the middle of April. During the fall, additional migratory waders, such as Tri-colored Herons, White-faced Ibis, Wood Ibis, White Pelicans, and Roseate Spoonbills, are common. The refuge has an active rookery in a cypress/tupelo brake on the Mingo Creek Unit. This rookery contains approximately 600 nests with a species composition of 65 percent Great Egrets, 32 percent Great Blue Herons, and 3 percent Anhingas.

Red-tailed Hawks, American Kestrels, and Northern Harriers are the most common raptors on the refuge and are observed frequently throughout the year. Other raptors which utilize the refuge include the Red-shouldered Hawk, and Screech, Barred, and Great Horned Owls. The Peregrine Falcon is often observed hunting shorebirds in April and from July-August. Bald Eagles frequent the refuge, particularly during the winter months as they follow the waterfowl migration. The refuge recently documented over 60 Bald Eagles utilizing the refuge.

Mammals

The most common mammals on the refuge are the white-tailed deer, gray and fox squirrels, swamp and cottontail rabbits, coyote, and armadillo. Furbearing species include the muskrat, beaver, mink, bobcat, spotted and striped skunk, raccoon, otter, and long-tailed weasel. Small mammals present are the eastern mole, short-tailed and least shrews, eastern chipmunk, various bats, cotton rat, eastern wood rat, cotton mouse, and harvest mouse.

Reptiles and Amphibians

A vast array of reptiles and amphibians utilize the numerous wetlands on the refuge. The most common snakes include the broad-banded water snake and the cottonmouth. Diamondback and yellow-bellied water snakes are also numerous. The unusual and interesting Grahm's crayfish snake has also been documented on the refuge.

The most common turtles include the red-eared slider and the spiney softshell. Alligator and common snapping turtles are also present, but less often observed.

Leopard frogs and bullfrogs are frequently observed as are Fowler's toads, green frogs, spring peepers, and chorus frogs. The spotted salamander, three-toed amphiuma, and lesser sirens have been documented on the refuge.

Fish

A large number of rough and game fish are present on the refuge. The most common species of rough fish include buffalo, drum, carp, and bowfin, while largemouth bass, crappie, several species of sunfish, and blue, channel, and flathead catfish are the more common game fish.

Threatened and Endangered Species

The Least Tern and the Piping Plover utilize the refuge during their spring and fall migration. These birds are usually observed feeding in various mudflats during July-September. However, these species have also been recorded during spring utilizing shallowly flooded fields. Additionally, Peregrine Falcons frequent the refuge and are often observed pursuing waterfowl and shorebirds.

Invasive Species

Nutria recently moved into the area and are causing considerable damage to refuge levees and roads from their burrowing activities. Armadillos also cause extensive damage to roads and levees by their burrowing. Wild hogs were first documented on the refuge in Spring, 2008.

Habitat damage from their rooting activity is extremely high and they will out-compete other resident wildlife for mast and other food resources.

Invasive plant and tree species include Japanese honeysuckle, Chinese privet, Chinaberry, and Mimosa.

Big Lake NWR

Birds

Bald Eagles are frequently documented on the refuge. They have nested on the refuge since 1993 and usually have one successful nest. Eastern Wild Turkeys are abundant on the refuge. Each year, hundreds of thousands of waterfowl migrate to the refuge, arriving as early as September and peaking between December and January. Canada and white-fronted goose numbers have increased in recent years, reaching more than 15,000 during January and February. The Baker Island wheat field attracts White-fronted, Snow, and Canada geese. Mallard, Gadwall, American Wigeon, Northern Pintail, Green-winged Teal, Northern Shoveler, Canvasbacks, Redheads, and American Coot are frequent visitors to the refuge. The refuge hosts an exceptional breeding population of Wood Ducks and Hooded Mergansers.

Great Blue Herons and Great Egrets are common throughout the summer months on the moist-soil unit. The unit also attracts Little Blue Herons, Green Herons, and Snowy Egrets. American Bitterns are occasionally seen using the area. Cattle Egrets utilize the grazed portion of the Ditch 81 levee adjacent to the West side of the refuge throughout the summer. Double Crested Cormorants continue to use the refuge in increasing numbers. Several flocks of migrating American White Pelicans use the refuge from late-February and March and again throughout the summer months of June and July. The most common shorebird is the Killdeer. Sora Rails and Solitary Sandpipers use exposed mud flats in the moist-soil unit. American Woodcock are often observed on the levee road. Other species observed include various tern species such as Forster's Terns and Spotted Sandpipers. Red-tailed Hawks and Red-shouldered Hawks are often seen on the refuge. Also abundant on the refuge are Great Horned Owls and Barred Owls. Other raptors include Screech Owl and Cooper's Hawk.

Mammals

Deer are abundant and the population estimate for the refuge and the adjacent state-managed wildlife area is 300 – 500 animals. Excellent habitat and a lack of hunting pressure contribute to high populations of raccoons. Fox squirrel populations remain high on the refuge.

Bobcats are frequently sighted numerous times along the Ditch 81 levee. Otters are thought to be abundant as they are often observed crossing the levee road from Ditch 81 to the refuge.

Fish

A large number of rough and game fish are present on the refuge. The most common species of rough fish include buffalo, drum, carp, gar, and bowfin, while largemouth bass, crappie, several species of sunfish, and blue, channel, and flathead catfish are the more common game fish.

<u>Threatened and Endangered Species</u>

Bald Eagles (no longer listed as threatened) have nested successfully on the refuge since 1993. Fat pocketbook mussels are found throughout the refuge and juveniles were restocked within refuge waters in the early 2000s.

<u>Invasive Species</u>

Beaver and nutria numbers are on the rise at Big Lake NWR. These two species cause significant damage to the refuge's forest communities and system of roads, levees, and water control structures. Feral hogs were released illegally onto the adjacent Big Lake WMA and have subsequently spread onto the refuge in recent years and are being spotted more frequently by refuge users. Their foraging activities are damaging the forest floor and the main levee side slopes north of Timm's Point.

Cache River NWR

<u>Birds</u>

Waterfowl

The Cache River Basin is widely recognized for its importance as wintering habitat for waterfowl. It is identified in the North American Waterfowl Management Plan as the most important wintering area for Mallards in North America. During peak years, 400,000 to 500,000 Mallards have been estimated to winter within the acquisition boundary of the refuge. While Mallards are the dominant species, Green-winged Teal, Northern Pintail, and Gadwalls are also common. Waterfowl numbers usually start gradually increasing from November to December, peak in January, and drop off significantly in February.

Wood Ducks and Hooded Mergansers are the primary species of waterfowl that breed on the Cache River NWR. Both are cavity nesters adapted to bottomland hardwood ecosystems. The Hooded Merganser is an uncommon breeding species in the region, and does not occur anywhere in large concentrations. By virtue of the extent of its remaining bottomland hardwood and permanently inundated wetlands, the Cache/Lower White Rivers' ecosystem is the most important breeding area for Wood Ducks in Arkansas; however, the secretive habits of the species have prevented the development of valid survey methods or population/density estimates. The large amount of mature forests and thus natural cavities, preclude the need for Wood Duck nest boxes.

Neotropical Migratory Birds and Resident Songbirds

Neotropical migratory bird species are experiencing long-term declines as a result of habitat loss across their full range of breeding and migrating habitats in North America and their wintering habitats in Central and South America. However, the proximate causes of the decline are not as clear, and evaluation of the problem is complicated by their intercontinental range and by the fact that this group of migratory species is composed of over 250 individual species within a number of different habitat guilds. As a group, resident songbirds are not currently exhibiting the degree of recent population decline documented for neotropical migratory species; however, it seems apparent that the 85 percent habitat loss in the ecosystem must have caused a commensurate decline in resident songbird populations and distributions from a historic perspective. Migratory songbirds that overwinter in the habitats of this ecosystem generally have not experienced population declines as dramatic as those of the neotropical species.

Neotropical migratory birds that use Cache River NWR are listed in Appendix G.

Marsh Birds

Secretive marsh birds include all species that primarily inhabit marshes (non-forested wetlands). Primary species of concern in North America include the King Rail, Clapper Rail, Virginia Rail, Sora, Black Rail, Yellow Rail, American Bittern, Least Bittern, Pied-billed Grebe, Purple Gallinule, and Common Moorhen. The American Bittern has been identified as a Bird of Conservation Concern by the Service due to the lack of basic population information. In Arkansas, population information on secretive marsh birds, such as status and distribution, is limited. Michael Budd and Dr. David Krementz from the USGS Arkansas Cooperative Fish and Wildlife Research Unit at the University of Arkansas have completed preliminary secretive marsh bird surveys in the Delta region of eastern Arkansas. Soras and American Bitterns were recorded at sites on, or near, the refuge in 2006. Both of these species were observed during spring 2007 on Cache River NWR in a Wetlands Reserve Program (WRP) impoundment and in a wetland located in a recently reforested area.

Wading Birds

Wading birds, such as Great Blue Heron, Great Egret, Snowy Egret, and Green Heron, are abundant in waterfowl impoundments, canals, bayous, oxbow lakes, and marshes throughout the year on the Cache River NWR. No known wading bird rookeries occur on the refuge.

Shorebirds

Shorebirds migrate through the LMV from the southern-most parts of South America to the northern-most parts of North America. They typically probe in soft mud (e.g., mudflats) and shallow water for worms and small invertebrates. In the LMV these birds generally move through during spring and fall, foraging as they migrate. They may only spend 10 days in the LMV, with very few overwintering or nesting in the LMV.

Quality shorebird habitat is also limited during the summer and early fall on Cache River NWR, since a majority of potential shallow water sites are in some form of cropland, moist-soil vegetation, or regeneration. The shallow water impoundments on newly acquired WRP sites, such as the Howell Tract, hold the most potential for shorebird use and management because of their diversity of water depths and mud bottom. Some shorebirds that occur on the refuge are Killdeers, Willets, Least Sandpipers, Lesser Yellowlegs, Black-necked Stilts, Solitary Sandpipers, Peeps, and Common Snipes.

American Woodcock

American Woodcock are migratory game birds that occur throughout the forested portions of the eastern United States. Woodcock populations in this region have declined 19 percent from 1968 to 1990. Population declines are thought to be the result of land use changes associated with land conversion and the maturing of forest habitats.

Cache River NWR contains a substantial amount of habitat that appears to be suitable for woodcock. Because woodcock hunting is not a traditional pursuit in Arkansas, there is almost no information available about the species for the state. Nevertheless, one would suspect that Arkansas' lowlands must be important migratory habitat given the large population which migrates to and is known to overwinter in Louisiana. The abundance of migrating woodcock on the refuge has not been quantified to date, but birds have been observed during pilot surveys.

Eastern Wild Turkeys

The primary resident game bird in the ecosystem, and one of special public interest, is the Eastern Wild Turkey. Being primarily associated with the mature hardwood forests of this region, turkeys once were distributed throughout the ecosystem. However, they are now generally restricted to larger blocks of forests, partly because those are most likely to contain a variety of habitats occurring at least to some extent on high ground. Turkeys utilize large blocks of open forest, young afforestation tracts, and open fields. The primary limitation to turkey populations in the more northern areas of the ecosystem, where the habitat becomes increasingly constricted along the watercourse, is the relative absence of forested lands above the 1- or 2-year floodplain.

Bald Eagles

During the winter, Bald Eagles are commonly sighted on the refuge, usually over open areas or bodies of water, while searching for prey. Eagles are found near large concentrations of waterfowl during the winter months on the refuge. Over the past 5 years, two pairs of Bald Eagles have nested near Rainbow Lake and near Opossum Creek. Both nests were constructed in the tops of cypress trees and each of these nesting pairs annually produced fledged eaglets.

Mammals

White-tailed Deer

The refuge consists of a mixture of farm fields, afforestation, moist-soil impoundments, and bottomland hardwood forests that create a mosaic of different habitats that provide for excellent cover and forage for white-tailed deer and other wildlife. Deer appear to be abundant based on general observations and harvest data. Deer herd health checks conducted by the Southeastern Cooperative Wildlife Disease Study (SCWDS) in 2007 indicate that deer on the south part of the refuge were in good physical condition and the herd was thought to be below carrying capacity. However, deer collected by SCWDS in the central part of the refuge showed signs of a higher population size close to carrying capacity, and SCWDS recommended reducing the population to a more healthy level.

Furbearers

A number of furbearers, including raccoon, mink, muskrat, opossum, coyote, bobcat, beaver, river otter, red fox, gray fox, and striped skunk, are thought to be common on the refuge. Beaver, muskrat, river otter, and mink are associated with the more permanently inundated wetlands and bayous. The raccoon is well-adapted to all existing habitats, and the opossum, coyote, foxes, and bobcat are more associated with drier forest and afforestation sites. Little or no formal data are available to provide population estimates for these species; however, general observations indicate that beaver and raccoon numbers have increased in recent years. These two species are of concern because of their high potential to negatively impact habitat and other wildlife species.

Small Game Species

Gray and fox squirrels are both abundant and distributed throughout the refuge where suitable, mast-producing forested habitat is available. Although they share habitats to some degree, gray squirrels are most common in deep woods, whereas fox squirrels prefer small woodlots and the edges of larger forested tracts. Their high potential recruitment rate (controlled largely by levels of available hard mast), high natural mortality rates, and other population processes would lead to the expectation that no significant long-term changes in their population densities within available habitat have occurred.

Cottontail rabbits and swamp rabbits are relatively common throughout the refuge; their numbers are largely controlled by the extent of available habitat. The rabbit population is usually higher in and around afforestation sites.

Black Bears

Black bears were once common in the Cache/Lower White Rivers' system before large blocks of forest were cleared for farming and other purposes. By the early 1900s, black bears had been virtually eliminated from the state except for a very small population, which survived in the most remote portion of the Lower White River. As a result of protection afforded by the refuges and state hunting regulations, black bear numbers increased significantly on the lower portion of White River NWR and surrounding forested area. Black bears are sighted on or near the Cache River NWR several times a year. Sightings are probably males passing though or juvenile males searching for a territory. Female bears, which determine population expansion in an area, are not thought to occur on the refuge with the possible exception of the large forested Biscoe tract on the southern end of the refuge. Bear hair-snare surveys were conducted in the Biscoe area by refuge personnel in cooperation with the AGFC during the summers of 2007 and 2008, to determine bear abundance and sex. No visits by bears were recorded. All bear sightings reported to the refuge office over the last 5 to 10 years have been maintained in a database.

Reptiles and Amphibians

The refuge's moist, forested bottomland hardwood habitat, bayous, oxbows, and impoundments are conducive for an abundant and diverse reptile and amphibian community. Numerous species of salamanders, frogs, and toads are present along with different species of turtles, snakes, lizards, and skinks (Appendix G). A detailed species list and associated habitat is lacking. A survey conducted in 2006 by the refuge biologist to detect amphibian abnormalities indicated that amphibians on the refuge were healthy.

Fish

Bottomland hardwood wetlands provide spawning and nursery habitat to many species of fish. Hydrology (primarily extent, duration, and periodicity of flooding) is one of the primary factors regulating utilization and reproductive success of fishes in wetlands. A total of 36 species of larval fish and 51 adult species was collected in a 1994 fisheries study in the flooded bottomland forest in the Cache River (Appendix G). Fisheries appear to be thriving in the Cache and White Rivers, Bayou DeView, and other bayous and numerous oxbows throughout the refuge. Among the fish found in refuge waters are various species of crappie, bream, catfish, bass, buffalo, carp, alligator gar, and paddlefish.

Threatened and Endangered Species

Ivory-billed Woodpecker

The Ivory-billed Woodpecker (IBWO) was once an inhabitant of forested habitats throughout the southeastern United States and Cuba. Although there are little specific population data available, it is likely that European settlement and the clearing of the forests caused the species to decline in the latter half of the 19th century. By the mid-20th century the IBWO was reduced to a very small population. The most famous study of these birds was conducted by Arthur Allen and James Tanner at the Tensas River in Louisiana in the late 1930s. The last widely accepted sightings were made in the Tensas area by Don Eckleberry in 1944. Since that time, there have been numerous unconfirmed sightings throughout the historic range of the species. Many of these sightings seemed highly credible but lacked hard evidence.

In February of 2004, Cornell Laboratory of Ornithology biologists became aware of reports of credible sightings of the IBWO in a portion of Bayou DeView, which is located on Cache River NWR. Subsequently, Cornell biologists and their partners documented the presence of at least one IBWO (Fitzpatrick et al. 2005) in that area.

A small stretch of the Bayou DeView was thought at one time to be providing some or all of the life cycle requirements for the individual(s) sighted on the refuge. Sixteen sightings of the IBWO were documented deep within the cypress-tupelo swamp of Bayou DeView in 2006.

Researchers from Cornell, with assistance from personnel from TNC, Arkansas Audubon, AGFC, and the Service, along with numerous volunteers, have been faithfully searching the Big Woods of Arkansas, including Cache River NWR, for the last several years. There have been many reported sightings, interesting audio, and other supporting data, but no additional video or still pictures have been recorded. A helicopter search conducted in February 2008 failed to produce any sightings of IBWO.

The refuge has been supporting the IBWO search team when and where possible. Cache River NWR's forester and wildlife biologist have been conducting IBWO Habitat Inventory and Assessment of the forest on the refuge to determine potential habitat.

Other threatened or endangered species that have not been found on the Cache River NWR but potentially could occur are fat pocketbook mussels, Least Terns, American alligator (listed due to similarity of appearance), and Piping Plovers.

Wapanocca NWR

Birds

There are 262 bird species known to visit the refuge. A large Great Blue Heron/Great Egret rookery (400+ nests) is located in the cypress trees north of the lake. Anhingas and Yellow-crowned Night Herons have also been known to nest in the rookery. A resident pair of Bald Eagles nests on the refuge yearly. Least Terns forage during the summer months over the lake. Snow Geese, once seldom seen in the area, now number up to 10,000 in the winter, attracted by the increased conversion of row crops to rice fields. During extremely cold temperatures in the winter, when most of the water bodies outside of the refuge are frozen, up to 100,000 ducks will flock to the lake. The majority of these birds consists of Mallards, but a great diversity of other ducks can be found as well. Large numbers of Shoveler, Northern Pintail, and American Wigeon can be found, as well as many diving ducks such as Ring-necked Ducks and Scaup. Wood Duck nest boxes (50) are maintained yearly to enhance production of Wood Ducks. Hooded Mergansers and mallards also nest on the refuge. White Pelicans have been seen on the refuge, as well as Great Blue Herons and Great Egrets.

Mammals

Beaver are common and have become problematic with their damming of the drainage ditches, causing subsequent flooding onto private adjacent lands. Raccoons also occur in abundance. A large white-tailed deer population occurs and is estimated to be over 200 animals in the winter.

Reptiles and Amphibians

Three venomous snakes are found on the refuge and include cottonmouth water moccasin, copperhead, and timber rattlesnake. An array of frogs and toads occurs on the refuge.

Fish

Historically, fishing on Wapanocca Lake was excellent as the lake was known as the premier bluegill and crappie fishery in the area. Good populations of catfish and bass were also found. Due to unstable water levels since the rehabilitation of Wapanocca Lake in 2004, fish populations have not come close to approaching historic levels. Currently, Carp, Grinnell, and Gar make up the majority of the fish population, with very few crappie and catfish being found. As water levels become more stable through restoration efforts, a more consistent fishery is expected

Threatened and Endangered Species

No threatened and endangered species are known to exist on Wapanocca NWR.

Invasive Species

Nutria were first discovered on the refuge in 1993. Nutria increase during mild winters and damage to cypress seedlings and levees are commonly observed.

Armadillo have moved into the refuge and it is suspected they have tunneled into levees and dikes, causing eventual failure.

Wild (feral) hogs are occasionally seen on the refuge, but populations have not yet become a problem.

CULTURAL RESOURCES

Bald Knob NWR

To date, no cultural resources surveys or inventories have been conducted at Bald Knob NWR.

There are however, numerous sites along the Little Red River and Overflow Creek that native Indians temporarily used. The Arkansas Archaeological Society documented several sites decades ago before establishment of the refuge. Prior to the establishment of the refuge in 1993, artifact hunters dug pots and surface-collected items such as arrowheads, bird points, and flint in agricultural fields scattered throughout the area. Most of the fields containing these sites have been removed from crop production and planted to bottomland hardwoods, which serves to protect the cultural resources that remain.

Currently, there are 18 historic properties recorded on the refuge. The majority of these are pre-Columbian archaeological sites, although several are 19th century farm or house sites. The now abandoned "Soybean House" is a square brick house built in 1925, and located in the northeast corner of the refuge. The Soybean House was documented during a county-wide architectural survey in 1986, but a period of significance was not identified. None of the archaeological sites have been subjected to systematic scientific testing or evaluation for inclusion on the National Register of Historic Places. However, the archaeological sites continue to be favorite targets for local artifact collectors and looters.

Big Lake NWR

The refuge has one major archaeological site located at the north end just south of the water control structures called the Zebree site. The site was excavated prior to the completion of the Ditch 81 project, and the artifacts recovered were catalogued by the Arkansas Archeological Survey. The Service is currently working with the Quapaw tribe to repatriate the remains at or near the Zebree site.

Cache River NWR

The Arkansas Archaeological Survey, under contract with the Corps, studied the Cache River and Bayou DeView in 1974. Field work associated with this project, which concentrated on the lower reaches of both drainages, identified 61 archaeological sites within approximately 1 mile on both sides of the Cache River and Bayou DeView channels. All discovery sites contained evidence of prehistoric Indian occupation, with the possible exception of one. The earliest evidence of man in the study area is from the Paleo-Indian period, circa 10,000 B.C. The majority of these prehistoric sites were located on natural levees, low-lying terraces, and low sandy knolls. In addition to elevation, the major factor determining the location and utilization of sites appeared to be soils. A strong correlation was observed between site location and areas of sandy soil with high natural fertility. These soils are all of the Bosket fine sandy loam, Dubbs fine sandy loam, and Dundee fine sandy loam types. In contrast, no sites were associated with the areas of sandy well-drained soils which have low natural fertility (Beulah-Bruno association).

There are several cemeteries dating to the late 1800s known to occur on the refuge. The remnants of railroad spurs that facilitated the first logging of the forests, which also date to the late 1800s, are found on the refuge. Additionally, an old railroad tram crosses the refuge and a steam-powered water pump which was used to fill steam engines also is located on the refuge.

Wapanocca NWR

A cultural resources survey was completed on the refuge by Northeast Louisiana University in 1978. Numerous isolated prehistoric and historic artifacts were found. Sites of interest were as follows:

Prehistoric sites
3CT139 – At least 125 X 50 meters, located at cooperative farmer temporary storage area and partially reforested.

3CT151 – 100 X 75 meters, located just north of the intersection of Ditches 2 and 3. Area was left to regenerate to trees.

Historic sites
3CT124 – 200 X 50 meters in the vicinity of the present day paved visitor parking area is associated with houses once occupied by the club's paddlers.

3CT127 – Small mound 150 feet west of headquarters building is believed to be the remains of a birdbath and garden.

3CT153 – Old club house which was located just west of the present day office building on the west side of the entrance road was demolished during landscaping and construction of the headquarters complex in 1980.

Regional Historic Preservation Officer Richard Kanaski conducted an archaeological survey around the margins of Wapanocca Lake during its drawdown in 2005. The main search was for pre-Columbian canoes, but none were found. However, the remains of three 20th century plywood flat-bottom boats were found, although they were not considered significant historic properties.

SOCIOECONOMIC ENVIRONMENT

Bald Knob NWR and Cache River NWR

The general socioeconomic setting of the Cache/Lower White Rivers' region is generally similar to that of the broader Mississippi River Delta, and can be characterized as follows: (1) Strongly agriculturally oriented; (2) low relative per capita incomes; (3) relatively high rates of unemployment; and (4) relatively low, sparsely distributed, and stable or decreasing population. Jonesboro is situated at the northeast edge of the watershed, and is by far its largest city with a population of 46,535. The other significant population centers are Brinkley (4,234), DeWitt (3,553), Clarendon (2,072), McCrory (1,971), and Cotton Plant (1,150), with numerous small communities of less than 1,000 scattered throughout the region.

Agriculture in the area is dominated by soybeans and rice, with a substantial amount of wheat grown on well-drained areas, lesser amounts of corn and milo scattered throughout, and some cotton production on the best drained, sandiest soils. Arkansas leads the nation in rice production (approximately 40-50 percent of annual national production), and the Cache River Basin significantly contributes to this total. There is also a relatively small but growing acreage of land dedicated to aquaculture production.

The forested wetlands and aquatic habitats of the basin have historically provided extensive wildlife-dependent recreation. The relative importance of hunting and fishing to Arkansans, as revealed in a survey of hunting and fishing conducted by the Service in 1995, can be illustrated by the following comparisons:

- Arkansas ranked sixth among all states in the percentage (32 percent) of its population which hunted or fished, 52 percent greater than the national average.

- The proportion which hunted and fished was 100 percent greater than the national average and the proportion that hunted was 150 percent greater.

Similarly, participation by residents of the Cache/Lower White Rivers and the surrounding region probably exceeded these statewide averages probably because wildlife-dependent recreation represents the traditional primary recreational opportunity in the area. Public use within the region is of intense interest to Arkansans for three principal reasons:

- The fish and wildlife habitats in the Cache/Lower White Rivers' ecosystem represent approximately 40 percent of all suitable areas for wildlife-dependent recreation in the Arkansas Delta.

- A significant proportion (65 percent) of the habitats in this ecosystem are in public ownership, with 89 percent of that being federal.

- These habitats retain very high fish and wildlife values relative to the remainder of the Delta (U.S. Department of the Interior 1995).

Big Lake NWR

Mississippi County was created November 1, 1833, of territory cut from Crittenden County and was named for the mighty river forming its entire eastern boundary. Osceola was the original county seat, but a second seat was added when Blytheville became the seat of justice for the northern section in 1870. The landscape of Mississippi County is flat, fertile, delta farmland with little forested acreage remaining. The economy is driven by and dependent on diversified farming and light manufacturing.

In 2005, the population estimate for Mississippi County was 47,911 residents. This represented a percent change of -7.8 percent from April 1, 2000, to July 1, 2005. The population was comprised of approximately 64 percent white and 34 percent black persons, with American Indians, Alaska natives, and other races comprising the remaining 2 percent of residents. Per capita personal income for the county was $22,958. The median household income for the 19,349 households in the county was $27,760. Persons living below the poverty level in Mississippi County totaled 22 percent of total residents in 2003. About 65 percent of county residents were high school graduates and 11 percent had a Bachelor's degree or higher.

Challenges common to most areas of the Lower Mississippi Delta, including Mississippi County, are long-term poverty, crime, teen pregnancy, and a lack of affordable housing. The town of Manila is located 3 miles west of the refuge and is the only town in Mississippi County experiencing population growth.

Wapanocca NWR

Crittenden County was formed on October 22, 1825, and was the twelfth county in Arkansas. In 2007 the county population was 52,103, with 80 percent of the population living in an urban setting and the remaining 20 percent rural. The county seat is Marion, but the largest city is nearby West Memphis. Like many Mississippi River Delta counties, the poverty level in Crittenden County is higher than the state average.

Crittenden County is part of the Memphis Metropolitan area, with most of its population growth being from families that work in Memphis, Tennessee, but choose to live in Crittenden County due to more affordable housing. Unfortunately, along with many of the families moving to West Memphis, much of the crime from Memphis follows, as the crime rate in the city is almost three times the state average, while Marion, just 4 miles to the north, is below the state average.

REFUGE ADMINISTRATION AND MANAGEMENT

VISITOR SERVICES

Bald Knob NWR

Bald Knob NWR has a public use program that serves an estimated 30,000 visitors annually. The most popular uses are consumptive ones—hunting and fishing. The refuge was accepted as Arkansas' 22nd Important Birding Area by the Audubon Arkansas Board on June 16, 2005. Since that time, wildlife observation and photography have increased significantly every year. However, there is no visitor services specialist on the staff.

The refuge continues to be an important area for graduate students to conduct research projects involving waterfowl and other migratory birds, agricultural and moist-soil production, resident species, and forestry studies. The refuge is open to the public throughout the year, except for November 15 to

February 28, when the waterfowl sanctuary is closed to all public entry and isolated to protect waterfowl and wintering eagles from disturbance. Most refuge roads, with the exception of those located within the waterfowl sanctuary areas, are open to the general public all year. Roads may be closed at any time due to hazardous or poor road conditions. All-terrain vehicle and bicycle access is permitted on established roads and levee tops on the Farm Unit and on designated roads on the Mingo Creek Unit. Horses, personal watercrafts, hovercrafts, and airboats are prohibited.

Hunting

Public land is the only place where many people have access to hunt and many hunters have expressed their appreciation to the refuge for allowing various types of hunting. Waterfowl hunting on the refuge has been successful and the majority of hunters are proud to have the opportunity to hunt on the refuge.

The refuge experiences large fluctuations in the number of duck hunters from year-to-year, as well as within any given year. The major contributing factors are the amount of water and habitat available for hunting in other areas of the state. When parts of the state are extremely dry, Bald Knob NWR has experienced over 150 hunters on several days. However, when the White, Cache, and other major rivers are in flood stage, the number of hunters utilizing the refuge is minimal, with many days having less than 20 hunters. The quality and success of a hunt is inversely proportional to the number of hunters on the refuge. Hunter success rates and overall quality of the hunt experience are higher when the number of hunters using the refuge is lower.

The refuge farming contract requires the cooperative farmer to pump and maintain a flood on the refuge's share of crops that are left unharvested during the month of November. The farmer must also pump and flood the acreage designated as moist-soil impoundments. In 2008, that acreage amounted to nearly 1,100 acres, which is located mostly (65-80 percent) in the waterfowl hunting area. In most years, additional acres are inundated because of leakage from canals and other factors.

The refuge allows morning-only waterfowl hunting seven days a week and hunters are allowed to use all-terrain vehicles. The hunters are allowed to hunt the fields (within the waterfowl hunting area) on a first come-first serve basis. Waterfowl hunting on the refuge follows the state season and bag limits. There is a possession limit of 25 shotgun shells per hunter and hunting groups must stay a minimum of 100 yards apart. Hunting from permanent blinds is prohibited and hunters must remove all decoys, blinds, boats, and other equipment daily by 1:00 p.m. Hunters are not allowed to cut holes or do any manipulation to vegetation, such as mowing, cutting, and weed-eating, or to hunt from areas of manipulated vegetation. Hunters are allowed to enter the refuge at 4:00 a.m. Commercial hunting or guiding is strictly prohibited.

Hunters are accustomed to these waterfowl regulations and for the most part there have been minimal conflicts. Most conflicts that do occur are during the first few days of the waterfowl season. This is especially apparent in dry years when the refuge has the majority of the available habitat in the surrounding area.

The refuge has allowed youth waterfowl hunts since 1999, and they have been received with much anticipation and enthusiasm. Approximately 10 – 20 different groups of youth hunters participate in the hunt in any given year and they have had varying degrees of success. The refuge intends to continue with this hunt. The value of this hunt is that it offers youth a positive hunting experience.

In 1999, the refuge incorporated a more liberalized goose hunt by allowing all day hunting for Snow Geese after the close of the regular waterfowl season in January. The waterfowl sanctuary remains closed until March 1, at which time it also is open to Snow Goose hunting under the state's conservation order.

All hunting on the refuge requires the hunter to sign and possess a current refuge hunting permit, which is found on the front of the hunt brochure. Numerous hunting opportunities are available on the refuge. Refuge hunts are summarized in Table 1.

Table 1. Hunting opportunities offered at Bald Knob NWR for the 2008-09 season

Deer – Archery	October 1, 2008 – February 28, 2009
Deer – Youth Gun	November 1 – 2, 2008
Deer – Gun Permit Only	November 8 – 9, 250 permits available
Deer – Muzzleloader	October 18 – 26, 2008
Squirrel	September 6, 2008 – February 28, 2009
Rabbit	September 6, 2008 – February 28, 2009
Raccoon	November 15 – 30, 2008
Opossum	November 15 – 30, 2008
Quail	November 1, 2008 – February 10, 2009
Waterfowl	State Season, Morning Hunt Only
Dove, Snipe and Woodcock	May be taken when seasons correspond with duck and/or goose season.
Turkey (Fall Archery)	Mingo Creek Unit Only – State Season

Fishing

Fishing begins in early spring and continues through fall. Most of the fishing activity occurs in the 80-mile network of flume ditches and canals throughout the refuge and on the larger permanent bodies of water such as Pole Brake. Approximately 7,000 fishing visits are recorded each year. Most anglers fish for largemouth bass, crappie, bream, various sunfishes, and catfish. Bowfin and drum are often caught incidental to the game fish. Most anglers fish with rod and reel from the bank around the numerous field drainage and irrigation canal pipes. Fish congregate around these water control structures, especially when water is flowing through them. To increase fishing opportunities, the refuge built and maintains seven boats ramps and associated parking areas. These areas provide access to Overflow Creek, Eagle Nest Brake, and Pole Brake, and consist of primitive dirt ramps as well as improved concrete ramps. Fishing activity is greatest during the crappie and bream spawning periods. During summer, most fishing activity is restricted to early morning and nighttime due to extremely hot temperatures.

Frogging is allowed and continues to be very popular, especially during the weekends. The refuge does not allow commercial fishing.

Wildlife Observation/Photography

This segment of public use is still relatively small on the refuge compared to hunting and fishing, but visitation to pursue wildlife observation and photography have steadily increased as the public becomes more aware of the opportunities that exist. There are nearly 100 miles of refuge roads and levees open to conventional vehicles that provide plenty of access for good wildlife viewing. These activities are especially high during the late summer/early fall when the refuge provides mudflats for migrating shorebirds. In addition to the shorebirds, thousands of herons and egrets use the shallow water and associated mudflats. Birdwatchers and amateur photographers from around the state converge on the refuge to observe and photograph these birds. Various chapters of the Audubon Society schedule field trips each year during this time to observe shorebirds, wading birds, rails, and other marsh birds. Audubon groups from Searcy, Jonesboro, Little Rock, Harrison, and other towns across Arkansas (and many from Tennessee) make at least one field trip to the refuge during the year. The refuge is known throughout the birding community as the best and most consistent area in the state for viewing wading birds and shorebirds. As waterfowl begin arriving in October and November, hundreds of birdwatchers and optimistic duck hunters also flock to the refuge.

Environmental Education/Interpretation

This type of public use is minimal. Local junior high and high school groups occasionally make field trips to the refuge. Professors at the local university also bring students in birding, herpetology, and biological classes to the refuge at least twice each year. The classes are generally small and contain less than 20 students.

Big Lake NWR

A variety of public uses occur on Big Lake NWR. Fishing and hunting are the predominant activities but wildlife observation, boating, and photography also attract quite a few visitors. The refuge is open to the public during daylight hours only. No visitor services specialist is on the refuge staff.

Hunting

All hunting on the refuge requires the hunter to sign and possess a current refuge hunting permit, which is found on the front of the hunt brochure. Hunting is allowed on the refuge for deer, squirrel, rabbit, raccoon, and opossum. Refuge hunts are summarized in Table 2. Hunter check station information is summarized in Table 3.

Table 2. Hunting opportunities offered at Big Lake NWR for the 2008-09 season

Deer – Archery	October 1 – December 31, 2008
Squirrel	September 6 – October 31, 2008
Rabbit	September 6 – October 31, 2008
Raccoon and Opossum (Hunt Only)	October 6 – 21, 2008

Table 3. Hunter participation and harvest data for Big Lake NWR's 2008-09 season

2008 Hunter Check Station Information			
	November	December	Season Total
Hunter Days	475	206	681
Antlered Harvested	6	0	6
Anterless Harvested	2	1	3
Button Buck Harvested	1	0	1
Totals	9	1	10
	Hunters	Hours Hunted	Harvest
Raccoon	6	24	4
Squirrel	12	125	25

Fishing

Fishing is the number one public use activity on the refuge. There were an estimated 20,000 fishing visits and 50,000 activity hours recorded for 3,200 acres accessible to anglers. Big Lake NWR and Mallard Lake, located on the adjacent state-managed Big Lake Wildlife Management Area, contain the only two major fishing areas open to the public in Mississippi County. Fishing pressure is usually heavy. Peak use occurs in May and June during the bream spawn. A fully accessible fishing pier is located at Bright's Landing and is well visited. Bank fishing access is provided off of two interpretive foot trails. Two public boat ramps are located on the refuge. Fishing is allowed throughout the refuge during March through October. During November, December, January, and February (waterfowl sanctuary closure), fishing is restricted to 200 acres south of the Sand Slough dam site and limited to non-motorized boats with electric trolling motors.

Commercial fishing is allowed under the same guidelines as for sport anglers. Commercial fishing permits are available for $25 each. Anglers must also abide by special conditions attached to their special use permit. The annual commercial harvest is calculated by compiling monthly commercial fishing reports, which all commercial anglers must submit as part of their permit conditions. There were four commercial fishing permits issued in 2008, and harvest was as follows:

2008 Commercial Fish Harvest							
	Buffalo	Carp	Catfish	Drum	Gar	Bowfin	Shad
Weight	4,600	3,200	280	28	160	40	28

Wildlife Observation/Photography

Vehicle, walking, and boat access allow for many wildlife viewing opportunities. Additionally, the Bald Cypress Wildlife Drive begins at the refuge headquarters and extends the full 10-mile length of the refuge to the northern boundary. The first 3 miles of this drive, to Timm's Point, is open year-round. A scenic overlook is located at Timm's Point, offering excellent wildlife viewing opportunities for waterfowl, wading birds, Ospreys, and Bald Eagles. Timm's Point and Bright's Landing have permanently mounted spotting scopes that offer wildlife viewing opportunities year-round. Viewing highlights include foraging waterfowl, eagle nesting activities, and white-tailed deer.

Interpretation

The refuge has three interpretive kiosks that provide users with information regarding refuge management activities, waterfowl migration, and refuge goals and mission. Interpretive kiosks are located at the refuge's visitor contact station, Timm's Point, and Bright's Landing. Inside the Visitor Contact Station, visitors can view interpretive displays of native fishes and archaeological artifacts.

Environmental Education

Students from nearby schools participate in an outdoor learning day at the refuge. Topics covered include the importance of the Service and the significance of Big Lake NWR for wintering and migrating waterfowl and endangered species recovery.

Cache River NWR

Cache River NWR has a public use program that serves an estimated 147,000 users annually; however, Visitor Services staff are lacking for the refuge. The most popular uses include hunting, fishing, other water-related recreation, photography, and wildlife observation. The refuge is in an active acquisition phase, therefore, isolated land tracts are scattered throughout the acquisition boundary making access to some tracts difficult. The refuge is open to the public throughout the year except for seasonal closure of the waterfowl sanctuaries, which is November 15 to February 28, primarily aimed at protecting waterfowl and wintering eagles from disturbance. These seasonally closed areas consist of six waterfowl sanctuary areas that include: Dixie Farm Unit (2,768 acres), Plunkett Farm Unit (1,081 acres), George Tract Unit (835 acres), Bank of Brinkley Tract (190 acres), Highway 145 (90 acres), and the Nicholson Tract (313 acres). Most refuge roads with the exception of those located within the waterfowl sanctuary areas are open to the general public all year. Roads may be closed any time due to hazardous or poor road conditions. All-terrain vehicle and bicycle access is permitted on designated roads and parking areas only, and only in support of priority public uses. Horses, personal watercrafts, hovercrafts, and airboats are prohibited.

Hunting

The refuge offers numerous public hunts. The most recent hunt seasons are summarized in Table 4 as follows.

Table 4. Hunting opportunities offered at Cache River NWR for the 2008-09 season

Deer – Archery	October 1, 2008 – February 28, 2009
Deer – Youth Gun	November 1 – 2, 2008
Deer – Modern Gun Permit Only	November 8 – 11 and 14 – 16, 2008 2,000 permits available
Deer – Muzzleloader	October 18 – 22, 2008 and December 29 – 31, 2008
Squirrel	September 6, 2008 – February 28, 2009
Rabbit	September 6, 2008 – February 28, 2009
Raccoon	November 15, 2008 – March 31, 2009
Opossum	November 15, 2008 – February 28, 2009
Quail	November 1, 2008 – February 8, 2009
Waterfowl	State Season, Morning Hunt Only
Dove, Snipe, and Woodcock	May be taken when seasons correspond with duck and/or goose season.
Turkey (Spring Firearms)	Hunt Unit I, State Season Hunt Unit II, Closed, Except Black Swamp Permit Hunt Hunt Unit III, State Season
Turkey (Fall Archery)	State Season

A current signed, free refuge hunting permit (found on the front of the hunt brochure) is required by all hunters participating in any hunting activity. In addition to the species listed above, beaver, nutria, feral hog, armadillo, and coyote may be taken during any refuge hunt by the use of equipment legal for that particular hunt.

Fishing

Fishing is an extremely popular activity on the refuge, with anglers targeting several of the 95 species of freshwater fish known to occur in the vast aquatic habitats of the Cache/Lower White Rivers' ecosystem. There are seven concrete boat ramps and 28 gravel or dirt ramps that provide access to the Cache and White Rivers, Bayou DeView, and numerous lakes located throughout the refuge. The most important fish to these user groups are largemouth bass, bluegill, crappie, and catfish. Peak use is during April – July.

A youth fishing event is conducted annually the first weekend in June and is open to youths 12 years old and under. The event is held at Miller Pond, which is stocked with catfish by AGFC, and is attended by over 100 youths. This event has been very successful and is supported by numerous local businesses.

Commercial fishing is allowed on the refuge and requires a special use permit and a $50 fee. Commercial fishermen are required to abide by all state regulations and special conditions attached to their refuge special use permit. Commercial fishing is allowed on specified areas of Cache River NWR in accordance with the seasons and methods listed below:

- February 1 to May 1 - all refuge waters except sanctuaries which open March 1.

- May 1 to October 31 - Cache River and all lakes, bays, and bodies of water accessible by boat from the main channel of the Cache or White Rivers.

- November 1 to January 31 - Cache River main channel only.

Only lawful tackle, as specified in the AGFC - Commercial Fishing Regulations, may by used on the refuge. Trotlines and snag lines may be used only in the Cache River main channel. Gill nets and trammel nets may be used on all refuge waters open to commercial fishing in accordance with AGFC regulations. Using seines, wings, and/or leads on the refuge is prohibited.

Wildlife Observation

Cache River NWR provides numerous opportunities for wildlife observation. Hiking one of the designated birding trails, canoeing, boating, or driving one of the many roads are the most common methods of observing refuge wildlife. Birding is one of the most popular forms of wildlife observation on the refuge. Viewing wintering ducks and geese, Bald Eagles, spring and fall migratory songbirds, and possibly an Ivory-billed Woodpecker are common pursuits for local and traveling "birders." Since the recent discovery of the Ivory-billed Woodpecker, the Cache River NWR has become a serious birder's destination. Two wildlife observation towers are planned, one on the Howell tract and the other on the Plunkett Farm.

Wildlife Photography

Although no official photography blind is provided, many visitors bring along their cameras for the specific purpose of photographing Arkansas' wildlife. Waterfowl, butterflies, wading birds, birds of prey, and other species are frequently photographed from refuge lands. The refuge is considering the possibility of installing photography blinds at several locations on the refuge.

Interpretation

The refuge has eight interpretive kiosks located at vehicle/boat entrance points to popular refuge tracts. These kiosks feature refuge maps, brochures, and educational displays concerning the various wildlife species found within the bottomland hardwood habitat on the refuge.

The refuge manager, law enforcement officer, biologist, office assistant, and forester conduct occasional programs that help to interpret the management activities of the refuge.

Environmental Education

Environmental education is conducted by various refuge staff members. Field trips to the refuge, guided tours, in-class presentations, and assistance with special classroom projects are examples of the types of environmental education offered. An environmental education component has also been included in most refuge special events such as wood duck banding or youth fishing event, and off-site events such as the Arkansas Birding Festival in Clarendon, Arkansas Lick Skillet Days in Brinkley, numerous Ivory-billed Woodpecker events, Earth Days, and Agricultural Education Days. The refuge visitor contact station also displays numerous educational exhibits such as animal skulls, hides, mussel species, mounted fish, and numerous other wildlife mounts.

Wapanocca NWR

The main portion of the refuge is open to the public during daylight hours throughout the year except when icy conditions make it hazardous to travel the levee roads. The 6-mile graveled Nature Drive and the Observation/Fishing Pier are located on the east side of the lake. The land north and east of Ditch 8 is closed December 1 – February 28, as a waterfowl sanctuary for Canada geese. This area is also where the crops are grown as forage for geese. Wapanocca Lake is closed from November 1 – March 15, to avoid disturbance to waterfowl using the lake. A Visitor Contact Station is located in the office building and is open 7:00 a.m. – 4:00 p.m., Monday through Friday (except federal holidays). A concrete boat launch ramp for Wapanocca Lake is located off Highway 77 on the west side of the refuge. Since the saucer-shaped lake is not conducive to bank fishing, three pull-offs/parking areas were developed on the lake side of Old Levee 1 to accommodate anglers without access to boats. The berm along the boat access channel can also be used for bank fishing. A fully accessible Observation/Fishing Pier is located on the east bank of the lake and is popular with the public.

Hunting

Wapanocca NWR offers hunting opportunities for deer, squirrel, rabbit, raccoon, opossum, and Snow Geese. Hunt seasons on the refuge are summarized in Table 5.

Table 5. Hunting opportunities offered at Wapanocca NWR for the 2008-09 season

Deer – Archery	October 1, 2008 – January 31, 2009
Deer – Modern Gun Permit Only	November 8 – 9, 2008
Squirrel	September 6 – October 31, 2008
Rabbit	September 6 – October 31, 2008
Raccoon and Opossum (Hunt Only)	November 1 – 30, 2008 March 1 – 31, 2009
Snow Geese	After February 28 until end of the state conservation season.

Recent harvest information for Wapanocca NWR is presented in Table 6 as follows.

Table 6. Hunter participation and harvest information for Wapanocca NWR's 2007-08 season

2007 Refuge Harvest Information			
Hunt Type	# Hunters	# Hunters Reporting Harvest	Animals Reported harvested
Raccoon (March)	168	27	52
Raccoon (November)	57	20	49
Squirrel (September)	180	55	151
Squirrel (October)	51	25	60
Rabbits (September)	1	1	1 (Swamp Rabbit)
Rabbits (October)	0	0	0
White-tailed Deer – Archery (October)	528	3	3 (2 Buck, 1 Doe)
White-tailed Deer Archery (November)	651	6	6 Buck
White-tailed Deer – Archery (December)	407	1	1 Doe
White-tailed Deer – Archery (January)	231	1	1 Doe
White-tailed Deer – Gun (November)	24	3	3 Buck

The Waterfowl Sanctuary north and east of Ditch 8 is closed to all public entry and use hunting and public entry.

Beaver, nutria, feral hogs, armadillo, and coyote may be taken during any refuge hunt by the use of equipment legal for that hunt.

Nontoxic (waterfowl) shot or rimfire rifles and ammunition only may be possessed and used for all small game hunting. The use or possession of buck shot is prohibited. Gun deer hunters may possess and use muzzleloaders meeting state criteria for deer hunting or shotguns with slugs only. Baiting or hunting over bait, salt or any attractant is prohibited. Dogs are allowed for rabbit, squirrel, raccoon, and opossum hunting.

A hunter information station is located at the entrance to the headquarters building. Hunters are required to sign in/out and record the number of animals harvested. A current signed, free refuge hunting permit (found on the front of the hunt brochure) is required by all hunters participating in any hunting activity.

The Round Pond Unit is open to hunting in accordance with state seasons and bag limits. However, it is closed to all migratory bird hunting. A Wapanocca NWR General Hunt Permit is required for all hunts.

Fishing

There is a big demand for fishing on the refuge since there are few public fishing opportunities in this area. Lake rehabilitation was first attempted with the draining of the lake in 1968, and reflooding and stocking of fish in 1969. During the 1970s, the lake was known as "the place" to fish for bream. Bass, crappie, and catfish were also abundant. Fishing visits averaged over 46,000 annually during the period the lake was open (March 15-September 30); visits exceeded 70,000 during one year. With the loss of the fresh water source to flush out the nutrient laden waters, the fisheries resource began diminishing in the 1980s. A total of only 20 fishing visits were recorded in 2004. Rehabilitation of the lake was again attempted with a drawdown beginning in 2004. Refilling began the fall of 2005 and the lake was restocked with bluegill (455,300), red-ear sunfish (95,000), channel catfish (56,250), and Florida largemouth bass (30,300). Fishing in the lake was not reopened until March 15, 2008, in order to allow the fish to grow and maximize reproduction. Efforts to obtain a secondary fresh water source will continue, since without it, the lake is expected to develop eutrophic conditions which once more diminish the sport fisheries resource.

The lake has not yet held full water levels since the restoration, presumably because rainfall amounts (the only water source) have not been sufficient to overcome percolation and evapotranspiration. Fishing currently is poor due to shallow water. A few people have tried fishing in Old Ditch 8 east of Old Levee 1 but had little success. Fishing is permitted on the refuge from March 15-October 31 in Woody Ponds, but this area has not been as heavily visited as the lake. Big Creek and other ditches which flow through the refuge are closed to fishing due to the presence of Dichloro-Diphenyl-Trichloroethane (DDT) and toxaphene at levels of concern. The taking of crawdads for personal use only is permitted. The taking of frogs, mollusks, and turtles is prohibited. The possession or use of yo-yos, jugs, or floating containers, drops or limb lines, trotlines or commercial fishing tackle is prohibited.

Wildlife Observation/Photography

Most of the visitors to the refuge for this activity are locals out to enjoy the scenery and the wildlife they can observe. The refuge is an attraction for avid birders because the varied habitats host a variety of birds. Birding is especially popular in early May during the peak of warbler migration. The 6-mile, well-graveled Nature Drive takes visitors through a wide variety of habitats. It starts at the refuge's headquarters and ends at the south side of the refuge. Visitors must turn around and come back out the same way. An observation/fishing pier and platform, accessible to mobility-impaired visitors, affords a scenic view of Wapanocca Lake. The use of these areas accounts for approximately 12,000 visits annually.

Interpretation

A visitor contact station, which is open weekdays when the office is open (except federal holidays), is located within the headquarters building, 1/8-mile east of the main entrance. It provides professionally installed exhibits. There are approximately 500 visits to these exhibits annually.

Central Arkansas National Wildlife Refuge Complex

Four refuges comprise the Central Arkansas NWR Complex, headquartered at Cache River NWR in Dixie, Arkansas, about 16 miles south of Augusta. The refuges are supervised by a Complex project leader and deputy project leader at this location. A number of employees are considered "Complex" employees because their primary duties are spread among the four refuges. These include a forester, biologist, administrative officer, and law enforcement officer. Each of the refuges has on-site staff. A short description of the staffing patterns for each refuge follows.

Bald Knob NWR

The staff consists of a refuge manager, engineering equipment operator, and park ranger/law enforcement officer. Facilities are limited to a government surplus mobile home used as an office and a small shop/equipment storage area. A farm headquarters, granary, equipment storage building, and shop are used by the cooperative farmer for refuge farming operations.

The refuge generally has adequate vehicles and equipment to meet the routine maintenance needs and can get specialized equipment from the Complex or other refuges if needed.

Big Lake NWR

The staff currently includes a refuge manager and an engineering equipment operator.

The office is a metal building and is located next to a small shop/equipment storage area. The refuge generally has adequate vehicles and equipment to meet the routine maintenance needs and can get specialized equipment from the Complex or other refuges if needed.

Cache River NWR

In addition to staff listed under the Complex discussion above, the staff at Cache River NWR includes an office assistant and two engineering equipment operators. Vacant positions include a refuge manager and natural resource planner.

The office is located in Dixie near Gregory, Arkansas, and is a former residence converted to an office. A large maintenance shop and heavy equipment storage is located behind the office.

Wapanocca NWR

The present headquarters building was constructed in the early 1980s, using Bicentennial Land Heritage Program (BLHP) monies. At that time, there was a permanent staff of five employees and thus the office was constructed to accommodate those numbers. The staff currently includes a refuge manager and an engineering equipment operator.

The buildings constructed using BLHP monies include the headquarters building, 4-bay vehicle storage building, maintenance shop, equipment storage building, and an oil house. A boat house was constructed by force account shortly thereafter. A Butler metal storage building was constructed in 2003.

The refuge has adequate vehicles and equipment to meet the routine maintenance needs and can get specialized equipment from the complex or other refuges if needed.

III. Plan Development

SUMMARY OF ISSUES, CONCERNS, AND OPPORTUNITIES

The planning team identified a number of issues, concerns, and opportunities related to fish and wildlife protection, habitat restoration, public use, and management of threatened and endangered species. Additionally, the planning team considered federal and state mandates, as well as applicable local ordinances, regulations, and plans. The team also directed the process of obtaining public input through public scoping meetings, open planning team meetings, comment packets, and personal contacts. All public and advisory team comments were considered; however, some issues important to the public fall outside the scope of this planning process. The team considered all issues that were raised throughout the planning process, and has developed a plan that attempts to balance the competing opinions regarding important issues. The team identified those issues that, in the team's best professional judgment, are most significant to the refuges.

A summary of the significant issues follows.

Bald Knob and Cache River National Wildlife Refuges scoping meetings were held on 9/24 (Bald Knob), 9/25 (Augusta), and 9/26/2007 (Brinkley) with 5, 10, and 7 people attending each meeting, respectively.	
Water Quality	With natural gas production in the Fayetteville Shale Formation increasing, there is potential for contamination of water bodies flowing through Bald Knob NWR from runoff, overflow, or breach of containment reservoirs for drilling fluids and tailings at the well sites. The refuge should develop a water quality monitoring program to document baseline conditions and monitor the water bodies over time. This will allow early detection of potential contamination and provide a baseline for comparison. The monitoring program could include water and sediment sampling, fish tissue analysis, and rapid bio-assessment techniques.
Water Flow Management and Bank Stabilization (Bald Knob and Cache	Numerous streams and bayous flow through the refuges. Due to the many changes in the landscape coupled with natural fluvial geomorphic processes, bank erosion and channel migration have and will continue to occur. In instances where these processes will not threaten buildings, bridges or other structures, it is recommended that they be allowed to take their natural course. If action is required to stabilize a bank, it is recommended that bioengineering be employed whenever possible. Expertise in bioengineering is available within the Service, state resource agencies, and local non-governmental organizations. Riparian vegetation, which is instrumental in strengthening and stabilizing banks, should be protected (and restored where absent). There is a section of eroding streambank on Bayou DeView in the Bank of Brinkley tract that

	was stabilized by using rock rip rap. This is undesirable for several reasons: (1) This material is not native to the area; (2) it is aesthetically displeasing; (3) it is expensive; and (4) if not properly installed will incur scour on the ends, thus requiring additional stone. In this particular instance, the streambank did not have trees or shrubs and a minor refuge road was close to the eroding bank. A possible solution to the problem would have been to move the road, protecting the toe of the streambank with natural materials while reshaping the bank and establishing woody vegetation. The use of bioengineering has been documented and has proven successful. Employing these techniques here will benefit fish and wildlife resources and make the refuge a showcase for innovative management.
Land Acquisition	Expand acquisition boundary to allow conservation and management of larger blocks of habitat for wildlife (e.g., swallow-tailed kite and neotropicals). Increase connectivity and expand from narrow corridor to larger blocks to increase interior habitat.
	Service should acquire private tracts to connect Bald Knob NWR to Hurricane Wildlife Management Area along Mingo Creek.
	On Cache River NWR, look at acquisition of sites outside 10-year floodplain to diversify habitats for biodiversity/species richness.
	Continue to acquire lands for Cache River NWR from willing sellers.
	Exchanges of refuge lands should be announced to the public.
	I support increasing refuge holdings and concentrate on acquiring lands to provide greater continuity of refuge ownership.
	Raft Creek and Zogt Hill (Rogers Bend) tracts would be better administered by Hurricane WMA. Bald Knob NWR?
	Move the acquisition boundary to include White River from Georgetown South.
Habitat Management	Research the potential role of fire in ecosystem management.
	Replanting old agriculture fields is a good idea.
	Controlling kudzu is beneficial.
	Forest management to benefit wildlife is a good practice.

Bald Knob and Cache River National Wildlife Refuges scoping meetings were held on 9/24 (Bald Knob), 9/25 (Augusta), and 9/26/2007 (Brinkley) with 5, 10, and 7 people attending each meeting, respectively.		
		Put in food plots (peas, turnips, clover, etc.) on Cache River NWR.
		Unharvested milo prevents seeing deer during hunts.
		Coop farming is a good way to provide wildlife food.
Hunting		Expand modern gun deer season (different times of the year) on Bald Knob NWR.
		Mow strips in reforestation areas for game bird habitat and hunter access.
		Allow the public to trap beaver. A special use permit could be required.
		Continue no trapping on the refuge except for beaver control.
		Allow all trapping but especially beaver by the public as the state does.
		Increase the gun hunt from 5 to 10 days.
		Spread the deer hunting days across the season.
		Normalize antler restrictions to be compatible with areas off the refuge.
		I would like no antler restriction.
		Limit turkey hunting to areas that have the highest numbers and close the other areas. Do surveys to determine turkey populations.
		Open the Dixie Waterfowl Sanctuary to hunting half-day, two days a week.
		Allow an all-day duck hunt on the last 3 days of the season, including the sanctuaries, which is comparable to the state.
		Make waterfowl hunting start times more consistent with White River NWR.
		Eliminate steel shot provision for small game hunting. Steel shot decreases killing effectiveness.
		The Plunkett Farm Sanctuary should not be closed during the quota gun hunts.
		Increase the quota gun hunt to 10 days or two weekends. Most only get to hunt on Saturday and Sunday, because many work through the week.
		Have more than a 5-day deer season.
		Allow hunting with dogs beginning November 15.
		Dove hunting should follow state seasons.

Bald Knob and Cache River National Wildlife Refuges scoping meetings were held on 9/24 (Bald Knob), 9/25 (Augusta), and 9/26/2007 (Brinkley) with 5, 10, and 7 people attending each meeting, respectively.	
Camping	We need camping areas on Cache River NWR.
	Allow camping on the refuge from 260 and north to Cavel.
	If the extent of the refuge is 70 miles, there should be 4 to 5 primitive campsites.
	Every tract should have camping even if it is only primitive sites.
	Add camping areas to the George Tract and Broadwater tract.
Access	Mow around long field behind Fitzwater so people can go further back.
	Allow additional access on Cache River NWR. More access to larger tracts between Highways 64 and 260 is desired. Reestablish previous roads (before refuge acquired) for access.
	Provide a continuous gravel surface of access roads in the George Tract and repair mud holes.
	Mow wider areas on roadsides on Beulah tract for safe travel and to decrease vehicle damage.
	Allow the use of ATVs to retrieve deer harvested by hunters from 12 to 2 o'clock without firearms.
	Only allow ATV use based on age or disabilities. No ATV use if not impaired.
	Need parking areas around Highway 260 (long field).
	Extend the Walker Access Road to AGF boundary.
	Remove stumps and cypress knees from Holder Access and Cache Bayou Access.
	Provide access road north of Cavell on East side.
	Improve access to landlocked areas.
	Make all landlocked areas sanctuaries (Lower Horseshoe) to prevent unfair advantages for access by adjacent landowners. Unless everyone can access the tract, it should be closed to public use.
	There should be more public involvement on road decisions (Biscoe Bottoms).
Wildlife Observation and Photography	Develop and provide unimproved foot trails in non-floodprone sites for birding opportunities. Delineate these trails on maps so visitors can easily find them.
	Provide maps of pedestrian trails/access for the public to engage in wildlife observation and photography.

Bald Knob and Cache River National Wildlife Refuges scoping meetings were held on 9/24 (Bald Knob), 9/25 (Augusta), and 9/26/2007 (Brinkley) with 5, 10, and 7 people attending each meeting, respectively.	
Special Programs for Youth and Elderly	Plan some events for the elderly.
	Provide more youth events (deer, duck, and dove hunts) at Bald Knob and Cache River NWRs. (2 comments)
	Have a 2-day Christmas deer hunt for youths. Add a dove hunt for youths.
	Implement a youth turkey hunt.
	Continue annual fishing derby at Cache River NWR. (2 comments)
	Generate shorebird programs for local schools to use for environmental education. (Bald Knob NWR)
Staffing	Add a visitor services specialist or interpreter to the refuge staff.
	Additional staff to properly maintain roads to reduce safety hazards is needed. An example would be the George Tract.
Communication with the Public	Notify all permit holders of meetings such as these (CCP scoping meetings).
	Make sure all public meetings are advertised in all local papers surrounding Cache River NWR.
	Have brochure boxes at all kiosks and keep them filled.
Law Enforcement	Increase law enforcement presence on Cache and Bald Knob NWRs by hiring more refuge officers.
Facilities	Replace current refuge office (old trailer) on Bald Knob NWR to better serve public contact and visitation services.
	Expand the equipment shed, storage facilities, and shop work area on Bald Knob NWR.

Big Lake and Wapanocca National Wildlife Refuge scoping meetings were held on 2/26/2007 (Manila) with 10 people attending and on 2/27/2007 (Marion) with 2 people attending.	
Public Use	We need a crawdad day at the refuge.
	Big Lake NWR is a resting area for ducks but a lake for fishing too. My grandfather was a commercial fisherman for 30 years on Big Lake NWR and I have fished it since I have been old enough. I have a 14-year-old son who I hope is able to do the same.
	I would like to see more opportunities for kids to enjoy Big Lake NWR, such as a youth deer hunt and youth turkey hunt. The kids are our future.

	Big Lake and Wapanocca National Wildlife Refuge scoping meetings were held on 2/26/2007 (Manila) with 10 people attending and on 2/27/2007 (Marion) with 2 people attending.
	Bowfishing would become popular if allowed on the lake and could help control the rough fish population.
	The refuge needs a walking and hiking trail enhancement, possibly a boardwalk.
	Add boat ramp for access to Ditch 81.
	Do not allow duck hunting on the refuge.
Water Management	Keep lake full of clean water where possible. Do not drawdown for any reason.
	We need a water control structure on south end of the lake. This would promote and/or allow water levels to be raised or lowered for both ducks and fish. This would also allow for channelization through the lake.
	Raise the water level 2 – 4 ". The lake has become at least 1 – 2 ft. shallower in last 20 years.
	Drawdowns should be controlled by the refuge to prevent muddy water and silting within the refuge.
	Dredge the channel from north end of big opening to south dam.
	Put water control structure on north end of ditch 28.
	I would like to see the problem with the lake silting in addressed. I am aware the Service has an agreement with the Corps to manage the water when drainage from Missouri is necessary, but the Service needs the authority to divert muddy water when needed. If something is not done, Big Lake will not be here for our children and grandchildren. This should the number one priority for the Service.
	I would like to see a decrease in the siltation of Big Lake. I have seen several feet of siltation which has completely filled in areas of the lake that at one time were prime fishing areas. If nothing is done, my grandchildren will not be able to enjoy the lake the way I have the last 40 years.
	I would like to see a major dredging operation done on the lake or at the very least, the main channel.
Habitat Management	Adding food plots in areas that are available would benefit deer and upland game.
	To save on mowing, add wildflower restoration on west side of the levee.
	Plant millet in shallow water areas for wintering waterfowl.
Land Acquisition	Increase refuge land if possible.

Big Lake and Wapanocca National Wildlife Refuge scoping meetings were held on 2/26/2007 (Manila) with 10 people attending and on 2/27/2007 (Marion) with 2 people attending.	
	I would like to see land bought as it comes available around and south of the lake. This would allow cover and habitat around the lake when floods occur. South of the lake, between the levee system, it would expand the refuge and add valuable cover and public enjoyment of the area the way it was before the clearing occurred.
Law Enforcement	I would like to see more enforcement on the area since there is a problem with night poaching and overharvest, mainly fish during the summer. Littering is one of the big problems that needs attention.

IV. Management Direction

INTRODUCTION

The Service manages fish and wildlife habitats and considers the needs of all resources in decision-making. But first and foremost, fish and wildlife conservation assumes priority in refuge management. A requirement of the Improvement Act is for the Service to maintain the ecological health, diversity, and integrity of refuges.

Described in this chapter is the alternative selected for managing the refuges over the next 15 years. This preferred management direction contains the goals, objectives, and strategies that will be used to fulfill the purposes of these refuges and achieve the refuge vision.

Three alternatives for managing the refuges were considered: Alternative A – Current Management Direction (No Action); Alternative B – Minimal Management, and Alternative C – Enhanced Habitat and Public Use Management. Each of these alternatives were described in Chapter III of the Environmental Assessment (Section B) of the draft CCP/EA. The Service selected Alternative C as the preferred management direction (Preferred Alternative).

With adequate staffing and budget, implementing the preferred alternative will result in strategic landscape conservation through land acquisitions from willing sellers, and intensifying and expanding current programs of moist-soil, scrub-shrub, and grassland management for waterfowl, shorebirds, other migratory birds, and other native species of wildlife. In addition, the refuges will intensify forest management to enhance forest health and wildlife habitat and will continue to implement afforestation and reforestation, enhance current wildlife management based on sound fish and wildlife management principles, provide interpretation and environmental education services for the public, and furnish additional law enforcement for protection of resources and the public.

Public uses can be allowed if they are appropriate and Improvement Act compatible with the mission of the Refuge System and refuge purposes. The identified wildlife-dependent public uses are to be given priority consideration, if found compatible. These priority public uses are: hunting, fishing, wildlife observation, wildlife photography, environmental education, and interpretation.

VISION

Refuges within the Central Arkansas NWR Complex will be conserved and managed as havens for migratory birds, especially waterfowl, in a region of the continent critically important for their survival. Working with partners, the Service will protect, restore, and enhance bottomland hardwood forest ecosystems, wintering waterfowl habitats, and other fish and wildlife habitats for the benefit of the American public. The Service will provide opportunities for the public to use and enjoy these refuges in a way that safeguards their values and promotes awareness of their importance.

GOALS, OBJECTIVES, AND STRATEGIES

The goals, objectives, and strategies presented in this CCP are formulated in the context of applicable statutory authorities, federal regulations, and Departmental and Service policies. They represent the Service's response to the issues, concerns, and needs expressed by the planning team, the refuge staff, partners, and the public and are presented in hierarchical format. Projects associated with the various strategies are identified in Chapter V, Plan Implementation.

These goals, objectives, and strategies reflect the Service's commitment to achieve the mandates of the Improvement Act, the mission of the Refuge System, and the purposes and vision of the Central Arkansas NWR Complex. The time scale for the implementation and accomplishment of the following goals, objectives, and strategies is the standard 15-year planning cycle for CCPs.

BALD KNOB NATIONAL WILDLIFE REFUGE

NOTE: All goals, objectives, and strategies described below for Bald Knob NWR are set in the time context of the 15-year planning cycle of this CCP unless otherwise indicated in individual objectives or strategies.

FISH AND WILDLIFE POPULATION MANAGEMENT

Bald Knob NWR Goal 1: Manage and protect migratory birds and native wildlife populations on Bald Knob NWR to fulfill the purposes for which it was established and to contribute to the mission of the Refuge System.

Discussion: Each refuge in the Complex was established for the purpose of providing for the needs of migratory waterfowl. Bald Knob NWR was created to protect and furnish feeding and resting areas for migrating waterfowl. Acquired as part of the North American Waterfowl Management Plan (NAWMP), this refuge provides a winter home for large concentrations of many species of ducks and geese, although it was purchased specifically for pintail management due to its identification as a major staging and wintering area for this prairie species.

Bald Knob NWR Objective 1-1: Migratory Waterfowl

Annually maintain current level of managed waterfowl habitat [17 million DEDs (duck energy days) and 3,125 to 5,050 acres of moist-soil, bottomland hardwood, un-harvested cropland, and harvested cropland habitats], flooded to a depth of two feet or less, in sanctuaries (November 15 – February 28) and hunted areas, sufficient to meet the habitat and population goals of the NAWMP as stepped-down through the LMVJV.

Discussion: The Mississippi Alluvial Valley (MAV) is an important ecoregion for migrating and wintering ducks and geese in North America. Bald Knob NWR provides important foraging and resting (sanctuary) habitats within the MAV for these waterfowl and serves an integral role in accomplishing goals set forth in the NAWMP.

Concern over waterfowl population declines in the 1980s resulted in establishment of the NAWMP, which focused the attention of federal, state, and private conservation groups on critical wintering and breeding areas. The LMVJV, which encompasses all four refuges in the Complex, was selected as one of the wintering habitat focus areas. One of the first tasks faced by the LMVJV was to develop a model or decision tool for determining how much habitat was needed, and a method for relating this objective to the population goals of the NAWMP. The solution was to consider wintering areas as responsible for contributing to the spring breeding population goals of NAWMP, proportional to the percentage of ducks historically counted in wintering areas (Loesch et al. 1994, Reinecke and Loesch 1996). In order to contribute ducks to spring breeding populations, wintering areas must provide sufficient habitat to ensure adequate winter survival. To quantify winter habitat requirements, the LMVJV had to identify limiting factors and made an assumption that foraging habitat was the most likely factor to limit waterfowl populations in the LMV (Reinecke et al. 1989). The process of relating habitat objectives for individual management areas to overall habitat objectives for the LMV involved several steps (Biological Review for Bald Knob and Cache River NWRs, USFWS 2008). Step-down objectives were established for Bald Knob NWR (Table 7). DED objectives were calculated by multiplying the acreage objective by the assumed DED standard developed by the LMVJV for that habitat type.

Table 7. Bald Knob NWR - Current migrating and wintering waterfowl foraging habitat objectives established by the LMVJV

Habitat	Objective[1] Acres (DED)[3]	Current Capability[2] Acres (DED)[4]	(+ or -) Acres (DED)
Moist-soil	500 (693,000)	660 (1,232,880)	+160 (+539,880)
Bottomland Forest	800 (100,800)	800 (152,800)	0 (+ 52,000)
Unharvested Crop	1,250 (15,777,500)	747 (15,662,526)	-503 (-114,974)
Harvested Crop	575 (386,975)	2,843 (286,465)	+2,268 (-100,510)
Total	3,125 (16,958,275)	5,050 (17,334,671)	+1,925 (+376,396)

[1] Acreage and DED objective provided by the LMVJV office.
[2] Current acreage and DED capability (has levees and water control structure, some have pumping capability) provided by refuge staff.
[3] DED estimates, calculated by using standard DED figures provided by LMVJV.
[4] Updated DED estimates adopted by the LMVJV Waterfowl Working Group in June 2006: moist-soil, 1,868 DEDs/ac; bottomland hardwood, 191 DEDs/ac; unharvested crop, 14,061 DEDs/ac (estimate based on actual acres of various grain crops left unharvested and flooded during the winter period); harvested crop, 287 DEDs/ac (estimate based on actual acres of various harvested grain crops flooded during the winter period).

Habitat objectives are based on food production and acres by habitat type for the complex of habitats including harvested and unharvested cropland and moist-soil areas. Each of these habitats is required to provide an important part of the food resources (i.e., native weed seeds, small grains, and invertebrates) required by waterfowl wintering in the LMV. Agricultural grains are high in carbohydrates, or energy (i.e., hot foods), needed by waterfowl to maintain body temperature during cold periods of winter. Native weed seeds (moist-soil seeds) and invertebrates provide high levels of protein and other nutrients used by waterfowl to complete important life cycle functions during winter such as molting, storing energy (fat) reserves, and improving overall body condition for the return migration to the breeding grounds and egg-laying. A variety of both natural and agricultural foods provide a diversity of nutrients for waterfowl with temporally varying nutritional requirements. Because of the high production of agricultural crops, unharvested grain provides much higher DED values per acre than natural seeds. For example, unharvested corn is estimated to provide 28,591 DEDs per acre, whereas native plant seeds found in moist-soil habitat are estimated to provide 1,868 DEDs per acre, and bottomland hardwoods with a 40 percent red oak overstory component are predicted to provide 156 DEDs per acre (Table 8).

Flooded shrub swamps and bottomland forests have some value as foraging habitats but may play a more important role by isolating birds during pair bonding, providing thermal protection on cold, windy days, and providing escape cover. It is critical that each component of habitat (i.e., agricultural grains, moist-soil seeds, and hard mast in wooded swamp/bottomland forests) be available if all the foraging and habitat needs of wintering waterfowl are to be met.

Table 8. Carrying capacity of selected foraging habitats of dabbling ducks wintering in the LMRJV[1]

Habitat type	Carrying capacity (duck energy days/acre)
Moist-soil	1,868
Unharvested cropland	
Rice	23,833
Soybean	4,677
Milo	18,046
Corn	28,591
Millet	5,203
Harvested cropland	
Rice	138
Soybean	36
Milo	480
Corn	505
Bottomland Hardwoods	
30% red oak	109
40% red oak	156
50% red oak	203
60% red oak	250
70% red oak	297
80% red oak	345
90% red oak	392
100% red oak	439

[1] These figures were recently updated by the LMVJV Waterfowl Working Group, and differ slightly from the values used by the LMVJV in the original planning process to develop waterfowl foraging habitat step-down objectives.

High waterfowl harvest rates and hunting activity in Arkansas identify the function of sanctuary or refuge as a key role in waterfowl management for Arkansas refuges. Activities such as maintaining body temperature, searching for food and roost sites, avoiding disturbance, molting, courtship, and pair bonding are energy consuming activities for waterfowl in winter. The assumed interaction between disturbance, energetic costs, and low survival can at least partially be mitigated by sanctuary where waterfowl can rest and perform these activities with a minimum of interruption. Sanctuary or refuge is critical for waterfowl to conserve energy to survive the winter period and conduct activities preparatory to perform other life functions, particularly reproduction.

Due to its strategic location in the heavily hunted MAV, coupled with the ability of this refuge to manage for a concentrated source of high-quality waterfowl food resources, Bald Knob NWR provides a critically important waterfowl sanctuary. This function must remain in place in order to provide areas free from disturbance to wintering waterfowl.

Strategies:

- Develop and implement a step-down water management plan to include flood dates and drawdown dates for all water management units.
- Provide flooded habitat (100-200 acres) for early migrating waterfowl, such as teal and pintail, beginning no later than September 1, and at least 50 acres for fall-migrating shorebirds (July through October), thus integrating water management for shorebirds and early migrating waterfowl to the highest degree possible.
- Flood additional acreage from November through December to provide food resources for wintering waterfowl.
- Provide a minimum of 7,745 acres of sanctuary from November 15 – February 28.
- By mid- to late-January, slowly decrease water levels in some impoundments to concentrate invertebrates for spring migrants, and continue this practice into mid-April.
- Monitor waterfowl numbers and habitat use by species annually to determine whether refuge and landscape-level (e.g., LMVJV) objectives are being met, and adapt habitat management as practical to meet objectives.
- Seek improved management strategies to increase food production and waterfowl use of food resources as practical.

Bald Knob NWR Objective 1-2: American Woodcock

Enhance American Woodcock foraging and roosting habitats on a minimum of 20 acres to contribute to the objectives of the American Woodcock Management Plan.

Discussion: American Woodcock are migratory game birds that occur throughout the forested portions of the eastern United States. Bald Knob NWR is within the woodcock management unit known as the Central Region. Woodcock populations in this region have declined 19 percent since 1968, probably due to land use changes associated with land conversion and the maturing of forest habitats.

In 1990, the American Woodcock Management Plan (U.S. Fish and Wildlife Service 1990) was completed, setting an objective to protect and enhance winter and migration habitat on public lands to increase woodcock carrying capacity. The plan also set objectives to inventory and monitor woodcock habitat and develop management demonstration areas.

Strategies:

- Assess and inventory woodcock habitat on the refuge.
- Develop and implement habitat management plans that provide preferred habitat for woodcock foraging and roosting, including thickets with high vertical stem density in the understory and fairly open ground cover on spongy wet soil (generally within 0.5-mile of openings), young afforestation areas, and agricultural fields.
- Create diurnal habitat in existing forest stands through thinning and patch clearcuts that also benefit other high priority bird species.

- Create and maintain preferred nocturnal habitat in wet agricultural fields (not fall disked) and wet "old field" (afforestation site) or grassland habitats of greater than 5 acres with exposed soil and patchy cover 1 to 3 feet in height.
- Manage openings of greater than 5 acres near areas of good diurnal habitat to provide nocturnal foraging habitat for woodcock.
- Take advantage of rights-of-way and other permanent forest openings to create woodcock habitat.
- Conduct evening flight counts, spotlight counts, or flush counts at least twice monthly from mid-November to mid-February, to estimate population density, migration chronology, and nocturnal habitat use.
- Restrict or eliminate fall plowing of crop fields since woodcock feed primarily on earth worms that are greatly reduced by late season plowing.

Bald Knob NWR Objective 1-3: Shorebirds

Annually maintain current level of 130 - 150 acres of shorebird foraging habitat flooded to 4 inches or less from July to October to contribute to the objectives set forth in the U.S. Shorebird Conservation Plan, Lower Mississippi Valley/West Gulf Coastal Plain Shorebird Management Plan, and by the LMVJV.

Discussion: Bald Knob NWR has the unique feature of a water control infrastructure that enables precision water management. This system has been used in recent years to manage water levels for shorebirds to create mudflats during the most critical time of year for shorebird migration, occurring in late summer and early fall. Shorebird management at the refuge began in 1999, and currently about 150 acres are managed for mudflats. Bald Knob NWR has become one of the most popular birding areas in the state, drawing in birders for the exceptional number of shorebirds that occur at the refuge during spring and late summer/fall. Several shorebird species found on the refuge are included in the Arkansas State Action Plan as Species of Greatest Conservation Need, including Piping Plover and Buff-breasted Sandpiper. Mudflat habitat also provides foraging opportunities for several species of wading birds and waterbirds, including Least Tern, Roseate Spoonbill, Tri-colored Heron, and Wood Storks.

According to the regional U.S. Shorebird Conservation Plan, the main limiting factor for migrating shorebirds is availability of foraging habitat. In the LMV, this occurs during the southbound migration (late summer-early fall) when water availability is limited. One goal is to provide mudflat habitat for southbound migrating shorebirds on public lands during this time period. At Bald Knob NWR, continued mudflat availability within the context of the ongoing cooperative farming program is needed for shallow feeding shorebird species.

Strategies:

- Maintain water in impoundments during spring and early summer to prevent vegetation growth.
- Drawdown water slowly in impoundments beginning in June until some mudflats are exposed, allowing natural evaporation to continue through September and concentrate invertebrates.
- Monitor shorebirds two to three times per week from June through September (using volunteers or other trained observers) to meet objectives of the LMVJV Shorebird Monitoring Program.
- Record water depths, vegetation, timing of flooding and drawdowns, and species of shorebirds utilizing various habitats to evaluate success in meeting objectives, and adjust management actions as warranted (i.e., adaptive management).

- Monitor shorebird responses to habitat conditions and management, and evaluate underlying assumptions of the regional Shorebird Conservation Plan by estimating the number of birds moving through the area and the rate and duration of migration.

Bald Knob NWR Objective 1-4: Colonial Waterbirds/Wading Birds

Annually provide 2,000 acres of foraging waterbird habitat, in conjunction with rice farming for waterfowl, and protect a five-acre rookery site from disturbance from March to August (breeding season) for long-legged wading birds to contribute to the objectives set forth in the North American Waterbird Conservation Plan.

Discussion: Bald Knob NWR provides habitat for breeding and wintering colonial waterbirds in shallow water areas and forested wetlands. Although this group of species is not a major priority for the refuge, management for shorebirds and waterfowl also provides foraging habitat for wading birds. Existing rookeries are surveyed annually and new rookeries are noted. Surveys should be continued to identify rookery sites, record breeding bird numbers, and estimate production. Rookery sites should be protected from disturbance, if necessary.

Strategies:

- In association with management for shorebirds, provide areas of shallow water and mudflat habitat that also will serve as habitat for wading birds.
- Perform surveys to identify rookery locations, provide rookeries protection from disturbance during the breeding and fledging period, and monitor production.

Bald Knob NWR Objective 1-5: Marshbirds

Annually maintain a minimum of 50 acres of tree-less wetlands with dense emergent vegetation at 40 to 80 percent coverage and open water from 20 to 60 percent coverage, flooded less than 12 inches deep to provide high-quality habitat for breeding and migrating marshbirds in conjunction with meeting waterfowl habitat requirements.

Discussion: Loss of freshwater emergent wetlands has occurred throughout the southeast as development pressures have increased. The King Rail is thought to have been seriously impacted and there is great concern over inland numbers of this secretive marshbird. The Least Bittern is another species of high concern. Marshbirds occurring on Bald Knob NWR rely on emergent vegetation, thus it is recommended that these species be taken into consideration when managing moist-soil units for wintering waterfowl and Wood Duck brooding habitat.

Strategies:

- Implement appropriate surveys and manage for marshbird species, including King Rail and Least Bittern, as feasible within the context of management for wintering waterfowl and Wood Duck brooding habitat.
- Identify marshbird habitat on the refuge and set back succession by mowing, disking, or herbiciding every 4 to 7 years to produce 40 to 80 percent coverage of emergent vegetation with little to no woody vegetation. Control willows, cottonwoods, and button bush on these sites with herbicide if they are too large to cut with a rotary chopper.
- Implement water management restoration projects where feasible to provide cattails and other emergent vegetation.

- Continue to survey secretive marshbirds, using playback calls during May and June in sites surveyed by Budd and Krementz in 2005-06, to determine species occurrence and population trends. Survey additional points as necessary to determine habitat use/preference. Use results of surveys to adjust habitat management activities as needed (i.e., adaptive management).

Bald Knob NWR Objective 1-6: Forest Breeding Birds

Annually provide sufficient habitat through forest restoration and silvicultural management to support forest bird species designated as high priority in the MAV (Bird Conservation Region 26).

Discussion: Recently, the LMVJV's Forest Resource Conservation Working Group has been working on the development of "Desired Forest Conditions" to benefit priority wildlife species in forested wetlands. Attaining desired forest conditions as outlined in the report *"Forest Restoration, Management, and Monitoring of Forest Resources in the Mississippi Alluvial Valley: Recommendations for Enhancing Wildlife Habitat"* will provide habitat to benefit a wide array of priority wildlife species, including high-priority breeding forest birds, such as Acadian Flycatcher, Prothonotary Warbler, Red-headed Woodpecker, Wood Thrush, and Kentucky Warbler. In brief, this report reviews the habitat needs of priority wildlife species and recommends "Desired Forest Conditions" at the landscape- and stand-level to enhance wildlife habitat. Additionally, the report provides several recommendations for improving reforestation and forest management activities. In addition to providing benefits to various priority forest birds, where possible, forest stand treatments should: (1) Stimulate the production of vegetation at the ground, understory, and midstory layers of the forest by creating openings of various sizes in the canopy to provide sunlight to the forest floor; (2) encourage development of emergent trees that rise above the predominant forest canopy; (3) retain large diameter class trees; (4) provide large standing, dead or dying trees; (5) contribute coarse woody debris to the forest floor; and (6) retain small diameter cavity trees. Forest management would provide benefits to priority Partners in Flight (PIF) forest birds, as well as a suite of priority wildlife species dependent upon forests.

In April 2000, refuge personnel established 41 permanent plots in the Mingo Creek Unit for conducting non-game breeding bird surveys to evaluate breeding bird and winter resident usage of forest habitat. The evaluation protocol was designed to correlate seasonal bird usage to forest habitat type to determine the "Desired Forest Conditions" discussed above. The survey points are located approximately 0.2-mile between stations. At each station, personnel conducted a habitat/vegetation inventory comprising overstory, midstory, and ground cover to determine habitat structure and evaluate possible correlations with bird distribution and habitat use. Counts at each location last 10 minutes with birds recorded separately for each of the three distinct time intervals of 0-3 minutes, 4-5 minutes, and 6-10 minutes. Also, the distance bands in which birds are recorded are defined as 0-25 meters, 25-50 meters, 50-100 meters, and > 100 meters with flyovers recorded separately. All birds seen or heard are recorded by distance and time.

The most common birds recorded include the Carolina Wren, Tufted Titmouse, Northern Cardinal, Blue-gray Flycatcher, Indigo Bunting, Yellow-billed Cuckoo, American Crow, and Carolina Chickadee. At least 50 different residents are recorded on any given year.

Over the past several years, reforestation goals have been met on Bald Knob NWR and additional new reforestation is unlikely unless land acquisition occurs. However, several modifications in management are recommended to benefit numerous non-game bird groups. Active forest management provides the opportunity to improve currently forested acreage to provide better habitat for high priority species.

Forest restoration may be considered in areas where land acquisition is a possibility. In the past, there has been discussion of potentially acquiring 5,000 acres that would connect Bald Knob NWR to the state-owned Henry Gray/Hurricane Lake Wildlife Management Area. If this opportunity arose, forest restoration in areas adjacent to forest blocks would increase forest block size to benefit more area-sensitive breeding birds and might reduce potential depredation and parasitism by Brown-headed Cowbirds. If additional forest restoration is considered, then placement adjacent to current blocks would provide, for a window of time, habitat for early forest successional species such as Northern Bobwhite and for forest-edge species such as Painted Buntings and Bell's Vireo. Over time, restoration would increase the current forest block size and improve connectivity.

Strategies:

- Maintain and increase where feasible structural habitat diversity in the overstory, mid-story, understory, and ground cover layers for priority breeding bird species with appropriate forest management techniques.
- Implement forest management techniques where feasible to provide and maintain more vertical vegetation structure to benefit forest birds, including species such as Swainson's Warbler, American Woodcock, Kentucky Warbler, and Wood Thrush.
- Where feasible, maintain at least 70 percent forested cover within a 10-km (6-mile) radius to reduce species vulnerability to nest predation and parasitism.
- Maintain scattered patches of understory to increase survivorship for understory birds in their first year and provide foraging opportunities for transient migrants in spring and fall.
- Continue forest restoration in newly acquired areas and link to other blocks of forest as feasible to increase block size and provide future habitat for forest bird species.

Bald Knob NWR Objective 1-7: Scrub-shrub or Early Successional Birds

Provide habitat, through forest restoration and development and maintenance of early successional habitat, for scrub-shrub bird species designated as high priority in the Mississippi Alluvial Valley (Bird Conservation Region 26).

Discussion: Reforestation efforts provide a recurring source of early successional habitat that benefits priority bird species dependent on such habitat. Where feasible, select sites to be maintained as scrub-shrub habitat through periodic disturbance. These areas should be allowed to revert to scrub-shrub habitat containing shrub, grass, and forbs species. Maintenance will be required about every 5 years through prescribed fire, flooding, mowing, or disking. Early successional species that would benefit include Bell's Vireo, Field Sparrow, Painted Bunting, Loggerhead Shrike, and Northern Bobwhite.

Strategies:

- Provide early successional habitat through reforestation of newly acquired areas.
- Identify and maintain appropriate areas in desired early successional conditions, using techniques such as mowing, disking, or prescribed fire.

Bald Knob NWR Objective 1-8: Grassland Birds

Provide up to 500 acres of nesting habitat, incidental to reforestation efforts, through management of old fields and reforestation areas (< 7 years old) for grassland birds designated as high priority in the MAV (Bird Conservation Region 26).

Discussion: Many high-priority grassland species are more prevalent at Bald Knob NWR during their migration and in winter than during their breeding season. These species, including LeConte's Sparrow, Lark Sparrow, Grasshopper Sparrow, and Loggerhead Shrike, use rice fields, moist-soil units, and old fields and therefore benefit from ongoing moist-soil management for waterfowl and marshbirds. Old fields and moist-soil units also provide winter habitat for Northern Harrier, Short-eared Owl, and Sedge Wren.

Strategies:

- Maintain moist-soil habitat that also benefits a variety of grassland birds.
- If feasible and desirable, create and maintain suitable grassland bird habitat on select old fields and newly acquired agricultural fields.

Bald Knob NWR Objective 1-9: Eastern Wild Turkeys

Provide and enhance habitat for Eastern Wild Turkeys, incidental to habitat management practices for trust species, and provide quality recreational opportunities.

Discussion: Eastern Wild Turkeys are popular with the public for wildlife observation/photography and for hunting. Turkeys are generally restricted to large, contiguous blocks of forests, partly because those are most likely to contain a variety of habitats. Such large blocks of forests are limited on Bald Knob NWR, as are turkeys. The Mingo Creek Unit, approximately 2,000 acres of mature hardwoods which is connected to an even larger forest block on Hurricane Lake WMA, contains the majority of the refuge's turkey habitat. Turkeys also utilize young afforestation sites and open fields. Hunting for turkeys is allowed only on the Mingo Creek Unit and is restricted to fall archery hunting.

Strategies:

- Implement an active forest management program on the refuge, with consideration given to turkey habitat needs where compatible with forest and open land management for trust species.
- Set harvest objectives, monitor harvest, and adjust as necessary and feasible in coordination with AGFC Turkey Biologist.

Bald Knob NWR Objective 1-10: White-tailed Deer

Maintain a healthy deer herd, with a balanced sex and age structure at a level consistent with long-term habitat capability, to prevent degradation of habitats important to priority species, and to provide quality recreational opportunities.

Discussion: Although not a federal trust species, white-tailed deer are of great importance to the public for observation/photography and hunting. Habitat on the refuge consists of a mixture of farm fields, afforestation, moist-soil impoundments, and bottomland hardwood forests, which create a mosaic of different habitats that provide excellent cover and forage for deer and other wildlife. Most refuge management actions aimed at priority species, such as migratory birds, also provide direct benefits for deer. Deer numbers must be held at appropriate levels through hunting.

Deer appear to be relatively common on Bald Knob NWR based on general observations, previous years' harvest data, and spotlight surveys. In the early 2000s, a partial deer herd health check was conducted by the Southeastern Cooperative Wildlife Disease Study (SCWDS) on the refuge. This survey suggested that the deer population was healthy and below carrying capacity. A new herd health check was conducted in September 2007, and indicated that deer are in excellent physical condition with the population below carrying capacity. Harvest over the last few years, based on refuge and AGFC check station reports, has been low. Archery season is open from October to the end of February and an either-sex harvest is allowed. An either-sex, muzzleloader deer hunt is open to the general public for nine days during October and there is a two-day, either-sex, Quota Gun Deer Hunt in early November. The Mingo Creek Unit is closed to deer hunting during the general gun hunt for deer. Specific population objectives for the deer herd on the refuge have not been established.

Strategies:

- Use public hunting as the management tool to maintain deer numbers within carrying capacity of refuge habitats.
- In coordination with AGFC, set harvest objectives, monitor harvest and population trends, and adjust harvests to maintain deer numbers at desired levels.
- Collect biological harvest data at self-check and manned check stations during all hunts in order to collect sufficient data to make inferences about the deer population.
- Assess herd condition/densities relative to carrying capacity by analyzing harvest data and interpreting density-dependent factors such as age-specific weights, antler characteristics, and reproduction.
- Determine current herd condition/densities relative to carrying capacity and past disease history every five years through herd health checks conducted and analyzed by SCWDS.
- Estimate population density or population index by conducting and analyzing annual spotlight surveys and monitoring long-term trends.
- Evaluate age structure and buck:doe ratio of deer population by analyzing and interpreting harvest data.

Bald Knob NWR Objective 1-11: Furbearers

Maintain healthy populations of furbearers consistent with habitat and population management objectives for trust species, and control nuisance animals when necessary.

Discussion: Raccoon, mink, muskrat, opossum, coyote, bobcat, beaver, river otter, red fox, gray fox, and striped skunk are thought to be common on the refuge. Raccoon are well-adapted to all existing habitats, and opossum, coyote, fox, and bobcat are more associated with drier forests, and afforestation sites. Muskrat, river otter, beaver, nutria, and mink are associated with the more permanently inundated wetlands and bayous. Little or no formal data are available to provide population estimates for these species on the refuge; however, general observations for the region indicate that beaver and raccoon numbers have increased in recent years. These two species are of concern because of their potential to significantly impact habitat and other wildlife species. Raccoons have the potential to impact populations of nesting birds and they also carry infectious diseases, such as distemper and rabies. Flooding caused by beaver dams and the blockage of culverts and water control structures by beavers are common. Staff time and funds are frequently expended to correct these problems.

Strategies:

- Monitor trends of terrestrial and semi-aquatic furbearers by conducting annual scent-station surveys.
- Trap and dispatch nuisance animals (e.g., nutria) opportunistically and remove beaver dams when necessary to protect refuge and adjacent private property and habitats.

- Consider opening the refuge to fur trapping if feasible and desirable by selected individuals or to the general public under special use permit to reduce the increasing cost of nuisance beaver control, reduce risk of disease outbreaks, and reduce predation on nesting birds.

Bald Knob NWR Objective 1-12: Small Game (Mammals)

Provide and enhance habitats for small game mammal species, incidental to habitat management practices for trust species, and provide for quality recreational opportunities.

Discussion: Gray and fox squirrels are common on the refuge where suitable, mast-producing forested habitat is available. Although there is some overlap in preferred habitats of these species, gray squirrels are more common in deep woods, whereas fox squirrels prefer small wood lots and the edges of larger forested tracts. Squirrels exhibit high potential recruitment rates (controlled largely by levels of available hard mast) balanced by high natural mortality rates and no significant long-term changes in their population densities within available habitat are expected. Squirrel hunting is popular during the fall and winter, and harvests are not considered to negatively affect the population. Forest management activities will maintain availability of quality habitats.

Cottontail rabbits and swamp rabbits are relatively common and are hunted in late winter. Their numbers are largely controlled by habitat availability. The rabbit population is usually higher in and around afforestation sites. Like squirrels, the reproductive potential is much higher than potential harvest and thus hunting is believed to be compensatory to other causes of mortality.

Strategies:

- Continue to allow the hunting of small game populations.
- Implement forest and open land management activities designed to benefit trust species that incidentally create and improve small game habitat.

Bald Knob NWR Objective 1-13: Bats

Provide and enhance habitats, incidental to habitat management practices for trust species, to support a healthy, diverse, and viable bat population.

Discussion: Several species of bats are thought to occur on the refuge, although no research or inventories on bats have been conducted. However, eight species of bats, including Rafinesque's big-eared bat, were collected on the nearby state-managed Rex Hancock/Black Swamp WMA during a research/monitoring project in the 1990s. Before management actions can be planned, a basic assessment of which species use the refuge needs to be conducted. Trapping/surveying for all species of bats on the refuge would be time consuming and expensive. Other alternatives, such as literature searches, would help initiate a species list. Target species or species of concern could then be focused on for more intensive monitoring, research, and management.

Strategies:

- Use published literature and other information sources to identify bat species that should occur in east-central Arkansas.
- Survey for bats in different habitats on the refuge using mist netting and assistance from universities and volunteers.

- Consider bat habitat needs such as roosting, maternal, or feeding areas while planning and implementing forest management activities for trust species.

Bald Knob NWR Objective 1-14: Reptiles and Amphibians

Provide and enhance habitats, incidental to habitat management practices for trust species, to support a diverse assemblage of reptile and amphibian species.

Discussion: Reptiles and amphibians are in decline across the southeast United States, due mostly to habitat loss and adverse modification of habitat. The White River watershed is a highly modified system as the result of extensive drainage, flood control, and clearing of forested lands for agriculture. These changes in habitat structure and hydrology have negatively affected the historic distribution and populations of reptiles and amphibians. Bald Knob NWR plays an important role in conserving remnant habitat, as well as in restoring habitat and ecological functions for reptiles and amphibians in a largely agricultural landscape. The floodplain forests, sloughs, and isolated wetland habitats are suitable for numerous species of reptiles and amphibians. No herpetological surveys have been conducted on refuge lands.

Amphibians are sensitive to a variety of environmental stressors and can serve as early indicators of environmental health conditions. Bald Knob NWR participated (2000-2003) in the Service's Abnormal Amphibians Study to document amphibian abnormalities in national wildlife refuge populations. These data indicated that the refuge had a consistent incidence of abnormalities in amphibians at a greater than background rate (3 percent). Such abnormalities are generally considered as indicative of the effects of chemical use on neighboring lands, although direct causal agents have not been identified.

Sampling also identified the occurrence of Chytridiomycosis infection in northern cricket frogs (*Acris crepitans*) collected from a rice field site. This infectious disease has the potential to cause significant declines in amphibian populations. It is unknown how long this fungal infection may have been present at this site and whether population declines due to Chytridiomycosis infections are likely to occur or have already occurred.

Approximately 6,000 acres of marginal agricultural land has been reforested on Bald Knob NWR since its establishment. Hydrologic restoration has been conducted on the Old Creek Bed associated with Overflow Creek, effectively re-establishing historic flow through the forested brake and eliminating the direct ditch flow, which was bypassing the natural system. These restoration actions should have significant positive impacts on reptile and amphibian populations of the refuge.

Strategies:

- Coordinate with partners (e.g., AGFC and State Wildlife Grants, universities, USGS-BRD) to conduct surveys for reptiles and amphibians.
- Maintain habitat connectivity to enhance reptile and amphibian movement between habitats, and aid in meeting their life cycle and resource needs.
- Restore and maintain hydrologic function in wetland and upland systems.
- Document the occurrence of Chytridiomycosis disease on the refuge through monitoring of amphibian health and attempt to prevent this disease from spreading to new sites.
- Periodically monitor environmental health of infected sites, with particular emphasis on those species most susceptible to lethal infections (e.g., *Bufo* spp. and adult gopher frogs).

- Coordinate amphibian health surveys with USGS National Wildlife Health Center in Madison, Wisconsin, and immediately report any die-offs or disease outbreaks.
- Do not remove adult or larval amphibians from infected sites for translocation to other sites, as this could result in the spread of chytridiomycosis disease.
- Be alert to the risk that collection of tadpoles and salamanders for use as bait in other areas can spread pathogens within and beyond the refuge.
- Continue stream flow restoration efforts for Overflow Creek historic channel.

Bald Knob NWR Objective 1-15: Fisheries, Mussels, and Aquatic Habitat Management

Provide and enhance riverine and floodplain aquatic habitats, and monitor fish and freshwater mussel occurrence and abundance.

Discussion: Flowing rivers, creeks, and bayous such as the Little Red River, Overflow Creek, and Big Mingo Creek represent one form of permanent aquatic habitat on Bald Knob NWR. Abandoned channel scars in the form of open-water oxbow lakes or forested brakes provide most of the permanent lentic habitats. These two forms of habitats may be seasonally connected to rivers during flood events. The frequency and duration of connectivity is dependant on flood stages, the elevation of the water body, and the operation of water control structures. Many fishes use the flooded forests, sloughs, and lakes as spawning and/or nursery habitat. Fishes, as well as freshwater mussels, use the rivers, bayous, and deep lakes year-round.

The aquatic habitats within Bald Knob NWR support a large diversity of species. Sport fishes are found in the rivers and the backwater sloughs and lakes. Some species popular with anglers include white crappie (*Pomoxis annularis*), black crappie (*P. nigromaculatus*), largemouth bass (*Micropterus salmoides*), spotted bass (*M. punctulatus*), bluegill (*Lepomis macrochirus*) flathead catfish (*Pylodictis olivaris*), and blue catfish (*Ictalurus furcatus*). Many non-game and commercial fishes are also found in the various habitats of the refuge. There are limited data regarding adult and larval fishes within the refuge. However, it is likely that many species occur in refuge waters as larvae, juveniles, and adults. Between 75 and 100 species of fish in the lower Mississippi River basin complete one or more of their life stages in bottomland hardwood wetlands (Killgore and Miller 1995).

Freshwater mussels are likely found throughout the refuge in flowing waters and to a lesser degree in permanent backwater sloughs and lakes. Specific information on the abundance, species richness, and distribution of mussels within the refuge is limited. There have been no known mussel investigations within the refuge.

The vast majority of aquatic habitats on Bald Knob NWR are representative components of a naturally functioning bottomland hardwood ecosystem, where few active fisheries management options are available. A major limiting factor in the spawning success of both riverine and floodplain fishes is the frequency and duration of flooding. A major factor affecting the survival of adult fishes on the floodplain is water quality and/or quantity in lakes. Many lakes may dry up or are subject to extremely high water temperatures and low dissolved oxygen levels during droughts. These factors are beyond the control of refuge management.

Strategies:

- Continue to reforest cleared land in the floodplain to provide more complex cover and forage opportunities for larval, juvenile, and adult fishes during flood events.
- Restore connectivity between rivers and floodplain lakes and/or forests where feasible.

- Modify operation of the Service-owned water control structure on Overflow Creek to allow seasonal fish movement upstream.
- Continue to restore stream flow in Overflow Creek to historic channel where feasible.
- Replace or modify when possible the function or operation of culverts or water control structures that prevent floodplain connections and fish movement.
- Work with partners to gather baseline data on fish and mussel populations within the refuge.
- Encourage researchers to conduct fish and freshwater mussel investigations within the refuge.

Bald Knob NWR Objective 1-16: Endangered Species and Species of Concern

Continue to support the protection and enhancement of endangered species through research, survey, recovery, conservation, and management programs.

Discussion: One goal of Bald Knob NWR is to provide habitat for threatened and endangered species. The refuge supports two species that are listed as threatened or endangered by the Service – Piping Plovers and Least Terns. Both of these bird species are seen with some regularity using the mudflat habitat. The state-managed Henry Gray/Hurricane Lake WMA, the south end of which is adjacent to Bald Knob NWR, may provide habitat for Ivory-billed Woodpecker. Although this species has not been documented at Bald Knob NWR, there has been discussion of purchasing 5,000 acres between Bald Knob NWR and Henry Gray/Hurricane Lake WMA and reforesting the area to provide forest connectivity. Providing larger block size and connectivity in this area through acquisition and reforestation efforts should be encouraged. Additionally, Wood Storks (although not federal-listed in Arkansas, but a listed species elsewhere in the southeast) are being seen more and more frequently in Arkansas during the spring and fall. Continued provision of habitat for these species, as well as other migratory birds, during critical fall migration periods from August to October is essential. Maintenance, improvement, and evaluation of the hydrology and water control structures will ensure continued use by these species.

Two delisted raptor species that use Bald Knob NWR include Peregrine Falcons and Bald Eagles. Peregrine Falcons are considered recovered after their delisting in August 1999, but their presence should be monitored. They are not a very common species, but can be seen during spring and fall migration and occasionally overwinter at the refuge. Outside of preventing potential harassment of this species and monitoring their presence, little needs to be done in particular for Peregrine Falcons. Bald Eagles were removed from the endangered species list in 2007. This species is still protected by the Bald and Golden Eagle Protection Act. Several Bald Eagles overwinter on the refuge, and are a popular bird for viewing during the winter months. The refuge has a pair of nesting Bald Eagles that have successfully reared young since 2000. Refuge personnel regularly monitor the nest and implement appropriate buffering measures to ensure adequate protection.

Strategies:

- Continue to monitor Bald Eagle use of the refuge and when nests are found, implement appropriate protective measures to minimize disturbance of nesting pairs and nestlings, such as a buffer area around the nest where seasonal entry is prohibited.
- Whenever Least Terns, Piping Plovers, or Wood Storks are observed on the refuge, note the conditions of the habitat being used and determine if this condition can be repeated in the future while ensuring actions necessary for waterfowl and shorebirds are still accomplished.

Bald Knob NWR Objective 1-17: Wildlife Investigations, Inventorying, and Monitoring

Within 5 years of the CCP completion, prepare and implement an Inventorying and Monitoring Plan that will improve and expand investigations, inventorying, and monitoring of the refuge's fauna to obtain sufficient baseline data to inform management decisions, determine if management objectives are met, and enable adaptive management.

Discussion: The Improvement Act formally establishes the necessity of monitoring the status and trends of fish, wildlife, and plants on national wildlife refuges. Service policy is to collect baseline information on key plants, fish, and wildlife to monitor, as resources permit, critical parameters and trends of selected species and species groups on and around Service units, and to base management on biologically and statistically sound data derived from such inventorying and monitoring (701 FW 2, Inventorying and Monitoring of Populations).

Monitoring, inventorying, and surveying (MIS) are very important means for scientifically managing trust wildlife populations and habitats, as well as meeting national, regional, and refuge goals. Before any MIS is started, the surveyor should seriously and honestly determine if: (1) Objectives, which are clear, specific, and measurable, are defined and can be practically met, (2) the results will actually be used to benefit the resource or make informed decisions, (3) quality and quantity of data needed to meet the objectives can be collected, (4) the MIS methodology is scientifically and statistically sound, (5) the costs of conducting the MIS are worth the results, (6) resources are available or will become available to complete the MIS, (7) the method of data analysis is pre-determined, and (8) MIS is prioritized so if resources become limited, then more critical MIS will be conducted.

Adaptive management is a system used by refuge managers to improve results by documenting management actions, measuring and documenting biological responses, and adapting (modifying) management actions to improve desired conditions/outcomes and determine if objectives have been met. Baseline inventorying and population monitoring at regular intervals provide data essential for informed decision-making by refuge managers and are fundamental for adaptive management. Inventorying and monitoring needs can often be met with the assistance of other Service programs and cooperative efforts with state resource agencies, universities, and USGS. Proper attention must be given to experimental and monitoring design, statistical procedure, and consistency in observation and data collection.

High-priority wildlife surveys include wintering waterfowl counts, waterfowl and shorebird responses to moist-soil management treatments, and forest breeding bird responses to forest treatments. Moreover, inventorying and monitoring efforts for adaptive management purposes should be expanded to include additional refuge resources that lack sufficient baseline data, such as reptiles, amphibians, bats, and mussels.

Strategies:

- Increase capability to conduct wildlife investigations, inventories, and monitoring by recruiting a biological technician for Bald Knob NWR and an ecologist and hydrologist for the Complex.
- Collect inventorying and monitoring data that contribute to assessment and decision-making regarding refuge wildlife management and facilitate adaptive management.
- Continue to coordinate with partners, universities, USGS, and others to conduct research, monitoring, and inventorying of wildlife resources on the refuge.

- Implement inventorying, surveying, and monitoring efforts for refuge wildlife resources according to the following relative priority:
  <u>High</u> – wintering waterfowl use, grassland and forest breeding birds, shorebirds;
  <u>Medium</u> – secretive marsh birds, abnormal amphibians, wading birds, woodcock;
  <u>Low</u> – white-tailed deer, wild turkeys, reptiles and amphibians, bats, furbearers.
- Strive to develop data sets that are statistically robust so that analysis of monitoring results can be more useful in determining adaptive management responses.
- Maintain inventory and survey data in databases that enable efficient data storage and retrieval.
- Record survey activity and results in annual narratives or annual survey plans.
- Recruit assistance with wildlife inventorying and monitoring projects from volunteers, such as interns, retirees, and/or skilled volunteers from universities or conservation organizations (e.g., Arkansas Audubon), when time, personnel, and expertise are lacking at the refuge.
- If possible, provide suitable housing for volunteers and interns as a means to effectively recruit the best candidates.
- Coordinate with AGFC, USGS, COE, NRCS, and other organizations to design and conduct research that will provide refuge managers with information needed to improve wildlife management programs to better fulfill refuge purposes.

HABITAT MANAGEMENT

Bald Knob NWR Goal 2: Protect, restore, and manage the functions and values associated with diverse bottomland hardwood forest and open wetland systems in order to achieve refuge purposes and benefit migratory waterfowl, shorebirds, and other native wildlife.

Discussion: Bounded on the south and east by the Little Red River and characterized by Overflow Creek, which winds through its middle, Bald Knob NWR contains a mixture of cypress-tupelo brakes, oxbow lakes, bottomland hardwoods, recently reforested lands, moist-soil impoundments, and agricultural fields. This variety of habitats supports a tremendous array of plants and animals, particularly migratory birds.

Bald Knob NWR Objective 2-1: Moist-Soil Habitat Management

Maintain the current level of managed moist-soil habitat, in conjunction with rice farming for waterfowl, to annually provide 500 - 650 acres of desired moist-soil plants (e.g., wild millet, annual smartweed, sedges, panic grass) producing > 500 lbs. of seeds/acre or > 50 percent coverage, that will provide a minimum of one million DEDs of waterfowl foraging habitat and meet the LMVJV forage objectives.

Discussion: The high seed production of moist-soil plants and their value as waterfowl foods have been known since at least the 1940s (Low and Bellrose 1944). However, managing seasonally flooded herbaceous wetland impoundments or moist-soil units has only become a widely accepted practice after many years of research in southeastern Missouri (Fredrickson and Taylor 1982, Fredrickson 1996). Today, more than 20,000 acres of moist-soil habitat are managed in more than 300 impoundments on state and federal lands in the LMV (B. Elliott, personal obs.). Although geese sometimes use moist-soil impoundments and eat shoots of germinating plants, rhizomes, roots, or tubers, the primary emphasis of moist-soil management is to produce seeds that will provide food for ducks. Regardless of the quantity of seed produced, moist-soil impoundments are highly recommended as a means of diversifying habitat (Fredrickson and Taylor 1982, Reinecke et al. 1989) and supplying food with nutrients not generally available in agricultural grains.

Suitable habitat can reliably be provided for shorebirds, waterfowl, and marshbirds by staggering the rotation among the existing moist-soil units. For example, a unit that is disked will provide mudflats for shorebirds during that first year, annual grasses and sedges for waterfowl during years two and three, and perennial vegetation for marsh birds during years four and five, at which time this unit could then be treated again to set back succession. This management action could be conducted only if woody vegetation does not become too large to disc or spray effectively to set back succession.

The current objective for Bald Knob NWR's 500 acres of moist-soil habitat is based upon a previously reported management capability. If this number represents permanent moist-soil acreage only, it may not be possible to meet it during most years. However, if the moist-soil acreage is considered in conjunction with rice rotation (set-aside), then the refuge is meeting that goal currently, with a combined acreage of 2,645 acres (1,995 acres of rice and 650 acres of moist-soil layout ground).

Strategies:

- Consult the manual *Moist-Soil Management Guidelines for the U.S. Fish and Wildlife Service, Southeast Region* (Strader and Stinson 2005) for guidance in management and evaluation of the refuge's moist-soil management program.
- Irrigate moist-soil units as necessary throughout the growing season to promote preferred plant production and reduce competition from pest plants such as cocklebur and coffeebean.
- Increase DEDs and habitat diversity if feasible by more intensively managing crop layout areas for moist-soil habitat.
- Acquire additional staff and equipment resources to: perform bi-weekly monitoring of vegetation to determine if management actions are needed, apply treatments such as disking, spraying herbicide, fertilizing, mowing, or flooding as necessary to control nuisance plants, and produce $\geq$ 500 pounds of seeds per acre.
- Monitor moist-soil management actions to determine results and efficiencies of such treatments on seed production and percent coverage of moist-soil plants in an effort to fine tune management activities to best meet objectives (adaptive management).

Bald Knob NWR Objective 2-2: Forest Management

Enhance the hardwood forestland complex to attain the desired forest conditions as described in the report *Forest Restoration, Management, and Monitoring of Forest Resources in the Mississippi Alluvial Valley: Recommendations for Enhancing Wildlife Habitat (2007),* as appropriate to fulfill refuge purposes.

Discussion: Currently, Bald Knob NWR contains approximately 4,000 acres of existing forest and 6,000 acres in various stages of reforestation. The largest block of forest is the Mingo Creek Unit, 1,800 plus acres. The Mingo Creek Unit, as formerly owned, was managed for timber production, and cut heavily reducing the red oak component. However, fairly desirable lower canopy development remains for resident wildlife and migratory birds. Other smaller forest blocks found on the Farm Unit of the refuge are less developed in the lower canopy and contain a higher component of oak. Some of these blocks are subject to long-term flooding or other altered hydrologic conditions and exhibit a significant senescence. Other blocks are permanently flooded tupelo/baldcypress brakes. Reforestation efforts began in 1996 and continued through 2006. Most plantations have excellent survival and growth.

The Forest Habitat Management Plan (FHMP) was written and approved for Bald Knob NWR in 2001. Continuous Forest Habitat Inventory (CFI) was implemented in 2000 and the inventory schedule is to collect data on a 10-year cycle to track habitat changes over time. The forests are evaluated under the FHMP through a 3-year evaluation cycle that allows active treatments and monitoring to be implemented on the same cycle. Through management prescribed in the FHMP, desirable qualities can be introduced in stands where they are lacking, or enhanced or maintained in stands where they are already present to some degree.

These qualities include:

- desirable vertical structure and levels of canopy openings,
- site appropriate species diversity,
- a sustainable proportion of desirable species in various developmental stages,
- a significant proportion of large trees with full crowns, and
- adequate availability of cavities and cavity-producing trees.

Generally, all marginal croplands that are acquired for the refuge are reforested. In recent years, much of the planting has been accomplished through carbon sequestration partners, or, in some recent acquisitions, the previous owner was enrolled in the Wetlands Reserve Program (WRP). The WRP lands often receive hydrologic enhancement in addition to tree planting. Most of the lands are planted with seedlings at 12 ft. x 12 ft. spacing, or 302 trees per acre. Much recent literature emphasizes the need for higher planting densities and larger components of soft mast species. The refuge relies on natural regeneration of soft mast or pioneer species, where available, but has incorporated these species on appropriate sites that are distant from a natural seed source.

The foremost threat to forest health at the refuge is damage from beaver impoundments. Historically beaver impoundments functioned within the forested system to provide wetland habitat needed and utilized by a variety of fauna. However, the surrounding watershed has changed and it is now mostly devoid of forests and consists of agricultural lands exhibiting altered hydrologic systems. This situation results in an abnormal volume and timing of water flowing into the refuge system. When beaver dams develop, the excess impounding of water during the period of tree growth is exacerbated by these unnatural inflows and causes tree mortality.

Wildfires are an additional concern; they can occur during the dry seasons. Most wildfires are either intentionally set, or they escape from adjacent field burning. Invasive plant species constitute an additional threat.

Strategies:

- Develop and implement Annual Habitat Work Plans (forest management prescriptions), using the FHMP evaluation/treatment cycle, to improve forest habitat and structure, promote growth of lower vegetation layers, and regenerate shade intolerant species.
- Conduct post-treatment monitoring to ensure that management objectives are met and to modify treatments to achieve desired results when necessary (adaptive management).
- Maintain the CFI system on a 10-year cycle and develop tools to analyze and track refuge habitats and site conditions over time.
- Note unique habitats such as cane, corkwood, and pondberry as encountered in CFI surveys for aid in future botanical surveys.
- Develop methods to streamline data collection and maintain practical measurements.
- Plant newly acquired cropland identified for forest restoration within 2 years of acquisition.

- Consider individual site geomorphology, historic and desired future conditions, degree of past site alteration, and hydrology in reforestation and afforestation sites to make decisions concerning appropriate species to be planted and methods of planting, and the timing, frequency, extent, depth, and duration of hydroperiods to be restored.
- Continue active dialog with carbon sequestration companies, USDA and other partners to establish adequate species diversity and stocking rates for reforestation and degree of restoration.
- Establish areas of self-sustaining scrub-shrub (e.g., plum, deciduous holly, sumac, and other native shrubs) within reforested blocks.
- Establish connectivity between larger forest blocks whenever feasible.
- Evaluate success of restored areas through the FHMP evaluation/treatment cycle.
- Cooperate with other refuges, AGFC, and NRCS to develop strategies to transition late-stage plantations into extant forest blocks by developing techniques to enhance vertical structure, species composition, and functions of a mature forest.
- Monitor greentree reservoirs (both extant and new forest) for impacts and long-term health to facilitate adaptive management.
- Strive to mimic natural hydrology on restored areas by removing to the extent possible existing levees or other obstructions to natural runoff, overflow, and backwater flooding without negatively impacting water control capabilities essential to other refuge programs.
- Maintain a shrub component along select, low-priority roads, ditches, and levees to discourage cowbird use and encourage use by other resident wildlife for cover and forage.
- Provide a recurring influx of scrub-shrub habitats.
- Consider geomorphology, hydrology, and soil characteristics to identify potential areas for cane restoration.
- Implement measures to promote and restore cane in existing forest such as thinning the overstory.
- Identify appropriate locations to restore sites to oak savannah, grassland, scrub-shrub, and other upland communities according to site geomorphology, historic and desired future conditions, degree of site alteration, and hydrology and implement various techniques, such as mowing or prescribed burning, to restore and maintain these communities.
- Continue wildfire suppression on the refuge by relying on local fire departments, the Arkansas Forestry Commission, and properly trained staff for suppression. Maintain firebreaks in young hardwood plantations throughout the grassy understory stage.
- Prepare and implement an updated Fire Management Plan that includes the use of prescribed burning as a habitat management tool.
- Administer the forest management program in compliance with 50 CFR 29.1.

Bald Knob NWR Objective 2-3: Cropland Habitat Management

Maintain the current level of cropland management, through a Cooperative Farming Agreement, to annually provide 750 - 1,000 acres of un-harvested grain crops (e.g., rice, milo, millet, corn) and a minimum of 15 million DEDs of waterfowl foraging habitat.

Discussion: Due to the extensive loss of natural habitats historically used by wintering waterfowl to meet their foraging needs, unharvested grain crops have become a critical component of properly managed wintering waterfowl foraging habitat since these provide a great quantity of food in a relatively small area. If these so called "hot foods" are not available, the suitability of a refuge for wintering waterfowl is decreased significantly. Similarly, for optimal suitability, refuges also must provide adequate sanctuary from disturbance. Due to resource and staffing limitations, the refuge cannot afford to force account farm the number of acres needed to provide the amount of grain forage crops required to meet refuge objectives. Presently, grain production is accomplished through the cooperative farming program in an effort to meet the foraging habitat needs of wintering ducks and geese. If farming conditions become unprofitable for the cooperative farmer, this critically important program could be lost. Therefore, every effort should be made to improve farming productivity and efficiency where and when practical.

Rice, milo, and corn are the top choices as grain forage crops for ducks. Rice is particularly resistant to decomposition even under flooded conditions and is high in calories. Milo and corn also provide high-energy resources for waterfowl and can generally be kept above the water surface, but problems often arise from depredation prior to flooding, as well as seed degradation after flooding. It is important to manage the cooperative farming program to provide a diversity of waterfowl foods.

As previously mentioned, the primary reason for establishing Bald Knob NWR was to provide a key area for those waterfowl species (Northern Pintail, Blue-winged Teal, Canada Geese) that need open-area habitats. The Biological Review team for Bald Knob NWR felt it was important to maintain a substantial portion of the total area in rice, milo, and moist-soil habitats to meet the primary purpose of the acquisition. A combination of rice, milo, and moist-soil foods provides the calories, proteins, and other nutrients required by these ducks for basal metabolism, molting, and migration.

As noted above, foraging habitat objectives set for Bald Knob NWR during the LMVJV step-down process and during the 1998 biological review are guides for the refuge's habitat management planning. Other factors must also be considered, such as the refuge's current and future ability to contribute additional foraging habitat. Much of the habitat management recommendations made by the 1998 review team for waterfowl have been achieved by aggressive management during the past decade.

A significant amount of refuge cropland has been converted to reforested fields in recent years. Approximately 2,850 acres at Bald Knob NWR has been taken out of grain production in the last ten years, resulting in about 4,500 acres (33 percent) being currently farmed through the cooperative farming program. Even with the conversion of significant acreage from croplands to reforestation, the refuge is still meeting its overall foraging habitat objectives, and approaching its minimum cropland DED objective of 747 acres of unharvested crops (Table 7).

The arrangement made with the cooperative farmer provides significant benefits that the refuge would otherwise not be able to provide. In addition to furnishing significant amounts of foods high in energy such as rice, milo, corn, and millet as well as moist-soil production, the farmer reworks levees, pumps water in agricultural fields, and conducts routine maintenance and replacement of all pumps and other equipment associated with the irrigation infrastructure. Approximately 2,300 acres is planted to rice on any given year, and fields are rotated with milo, soybeans, millet, corn, and moist-soil production.

The cooperator's share from the total rice acreage is 75 percent and the refuge's share is 25 percent. None of the soybean acreage is kept by the refuge. Instead, the refuge's share is swapped for milo, millet, moist-soil, and occasional corn, all of which are left in the field unharvested to provide supplemental food resources for wintering waterfowl and other native wildlife. Generally, half of the rice field acreage is prepared the summer before it is to be aerially planted and consequently left fallow for the majority of the growing season. These "set aside" fields are allowed to germinate and produce moist-soil plants the remainder of the growing season and are inundated during the fall and winter months. The following spring, rice is aerially seeded into the flooded field. This practice provides large acreages of excellent moist-soil foods such as smartweed, millet, residual rice, and various grasses, which are also heavily utilized by wintering waterfowl.

Shorebird management has been a high priority at Bald Knob NWR over the last 8 to 10 years. Rice farming is preferred over moist-soil management to achieve shorebird habitat objectives. Annual conversion of fallow fields to rice production coincides with early shorebird migration. Rice stubble provides the critical substrate necessary to sustain invertebrates which are so vital to shorebirds during their late summer/early fall migration. Deep water in shorebird managed fields is supplied by the cooperative farmer until early July, at which time it is slowly drained to provide critical mudflat habitat, which lasts until mid-September. This management practice also provides much needed shallow water habitat for Northern Pintail and Blue-winged Teal during this time. Water could also be pumped on selected fields to create mudflats and shallow water habitat for waterfowl. It is imperative that the cooperative farming program continue to provide foraging and overwintering needs of waterfowl, shorebirds, and other migratory birds.

In addition to use by wintering ducks, substantial numbers of Snow and White-fronted Geese have utilized refuge crop fields in recent years. In order to at least partially meet the foraging requirements of these geese, the DED objectives should be recognized as _minimal_ requirements.

Strategies:

- Use cooperative farming as an effective and valuable tool for meeting waterfowl and shorebird foraging habitat objectives, including preventing habitat succession in the moist-soil units to promote growth of desired annual plants.
- Continue to prepare half of the rice field acreage the summer before it is to be planted and leave fallow for the majority of the growing season to provide additional acreage of excellent moist-soil foods that are heavily utilized by wintering waterfowl.
- Ensure that the cooperative farmer supplies deep water in fields managed for shorebirds until mid-July then slowly drains these fields to provide mudflat habitat that remains into mid-September.
- Consider pumping water on selected fields if desirable to create additional acreage of mudflats and shallow water habitat for shorebirds.
- Maintain adequate records of agricultural actions, crop rotations, habitat conditions, and species' responses, and modify methods as needed to meet objectives (adaptive management).
- Administer the cooperative farming program in compliance with 50 CFR 29.1.

Bald Knob NWR Objective 2-4: Water Management

Continue to restore or enhance the hydrologic regime of the refuge, utilizing low-maintenance water delivery systems and natural processes where feasible, to improve cropland, moist-soil, and other wetland management units that provide critical habitat resources for wetland-dependent species.

Discussion: Management of water levels, flows, and quantities is a major focus of the refuge's active habitat management. Water control infrastructure (e.g., levees, ditches, wells, pumps, water control structures) should be evaluated for all wetland management units to determine: (1) Physical condition, (2) size and capacity to efficiently move water in and out of units, (3) type of structure, (e.g., screw-gate, flash-board riser) and whether it is efficient and appropriate, (4) proper location, and (5) ability to manage for desired water depth, timing, and duration. Management should strive to achieve independent flood and drain capabilities for all units.

Because cooperative farmers perform some water management under the direct supervision of the refuge manager, maintenance and operation of the structures should be clearly detailed and be regularly monitored.

Many areas of Bald Knob NWR have been reforested with bottomland hardwood species, many of which are relatively intolerant of growing season flooding. Certain sites have the potential conversion to greentree reservoirs (GTR). However, experience with GTRs in the MAV documents that such sites must be carefully managed to emulate natural dynamics of flooding and draining.

Some infrastructure has the capability of allowing some relatively natural overbank flooding into reforested sites, but as with GTRs, management plans must be carefully designed to emulate natural dynamics of flooding related to elevation, geomorphic surface, soils, and bottomland hardwood community type. A careful evaluation of existing infrastructure is needed to determine constraints and opportunities for simulating such flooding regimes.

Some sites on Bald Knob NWR have physical constraints to natural water flow patterns, especially efficient drainage following flooding, whether natural, beaver, or man-caused. All potential natural flow patterns on the refuge should be identified, and where possible, obstructions to natural flow patterns should be removed, or at least be modified so that prolonged growing season flooding does not occur, especially in bottomland hardwood sites. This restoration includes removing unneeded roads, levees, ditches, and berms along with restoration of sloughs, swales, and other topographic features.

Strategies:

- Develop and implement a detailed water management plan to enable proper management of all refuge wetland habitats.
- Maintain and improve the water control infrastructure to manage the moist-soil/farm units.
- Manage moist-soil/farm units for a rotational complex of habitats, water depths, time of flooding, and desired vegetation communities consistent with climate, soil, and topographic features of the refuge.
- Develop water control infrastructure necessary to provide short duration, and annually dynamic seasonal flooding regimes in reforested areas.
- Improve drainage capabilities for all bottomland forest and reforested sites subject to overbank flooding from local drainage systems, and for sites where constraints to natural flow patterns occur from activities on-site or adjacent lands.
- Coordinate with Arkansas Ecological Services Field Office, Arkansas Department of Environmental Quality, and USGS to establish additional water monitoring at creeks, streams, and ditches that flow on or across refuge lands.
- Recruit a hydrologist based at Big Lake NWR to coordinate hydrological and water quality issues on all refuges within the Complex, and to coordinate hydrological research and monitoring, provide technical advice to adjacent landowners, provide liaison function with COE, and coordinate aquatic restoration projects.

Bald Knob NWR Objective 2-5: Habitat Investigations, Inventorying, and Monitoring

Within 5 years of the CCP completion, prepare and implement an Inventorying and Monitoring Plan (IMP) that will improve and expand investigations, inventorying, and monitoring of the refuge's wildlife habitat and use to obtain sufficient baseline data to inform management decisions, determine if management objectives are met, and enable adaptive management.

Discussion: The Improvement Act formally establishes the necessity of monitoring the status and trends of fish, wildlife, and plants on national wildlife refuges. Service policy is to collect baseline information on key plants, fish, and wildlife to monitor, as resources permit, critical parameters and trends of selected species and species groups on and around Service units, and to base management on biologically and statistically sound data derived from such inventorying and monitoring (701 FW 2, Inventorying and Monitoring of Populations).

Monitoring, inventorying, and surveying (MIS) are a very important means for scientifically managing trust wildlife populations and habitat as well as meeting national, regional, and refuge goals. Before any MIS is started, the surveyor should seriously and honestly determine if: (1) Objectives, which are clear, specific, and measurable, are defined and can be practically met, (2) the results will actually be used to benefit the resource or make informed decisions, (3) quality and quantity of data needed to meet the objectives can be collected, (4) the MIS methodology is scientifically and statistically sound, (5) the costs of conducting the MIS are worth the results, (6) resources are available or will become available to complete the MIS, (7) the method of data analysis is pre-determined, and (8) MIS is prioritized so if resources become limited then more critical MIS will be conducted.

Adaptive management is a system used by refuge managers to improve results by documenting management actions, measuring and documenting biological responses, and adapting (modifying) management actions to improve desired conditions/outcomes and determine if objectives have been met. Baseline inventorying and monitoring at regular intervals provide data essential for informed decision-making by refuge managers. Appropriate inventorying and pre- and post-treatment monitoring of refuge habitats are fundamental for adaptive management. Inventorying and monitoring needs can often be met with the assistance of other Service programs and cooperative efforts with state resource agencies, universities, and USGS. Proper attention must be given to experimental and monitoring design, statistical procedure, and consistency in observation and data collection.

Management of moist-soil sites in particular requires intensive monitoring throughout establishment and manipulation periods to assure that sufficient waterfowl and shorebird foods are produced to meet habitat goals. Responses to management actions by moist-soil plants varies highly due to specific treatment conditions, and monitoring is conducted in an attempt to document treatment/response relationships and duplicate such conditions in sequential years. While water gauges in each impoundment allow detailed records on water levels, data on soil moisture, plant germination, and composition also will be required to successfully manage moist-soil areas.

Strategies:
- Increase capability to conduct habitat investigations, inventories, and monitoring by recruiting a biological technician for Bald Knob NWR and an ecologist, hydrologist, assistant forester, and forestry technician for the Central Arkansas NWR Complex.
- Collect and assess inventorying and monitoring data that are relevant to and contribute to decision-making regarding refuge habitat management (adaptive management).
- Continue to coordinate with partners, universities, USGS, and others to conduct research, monitoring, and inventorying of habitat resources on the refuge.
- Implement inventorying and monitoring efforts for refuge habitat resources including moist-soil units, continuous forest inventory (CFI) plots, botanical surveys, vegetation responses to management activities, invasive plant infestations, hard mast production, success of afforestation and reforestation activities, cropland habitat production, and plant species composition of grassland, scrub-shrub, and early successional habitats.
- Maintain habitat inventory and survey data in databases that enable efficient data storage and retrieval.

- Strive to develop data sets that are statistically robust so that analysis of monitoring results can be more useful in determining adaptive management responses if objectives are not being accomplished.
- Record survey activity and results in annual narratives or annual habitat and survey plans.
- When time, personnel, or expertise are lacking, recruit volunteers, such as interns, retirees, and/or skilled volunteers from universities or conservation clubs (e.g., Arkansas Audubon), to assist with habitat inventory and monitoring.
- If possible provide suitable housing for volunteers and interns as a means to effectively recruit the best candidates.
- Continue to enhance refuge inventory and mapping capabilities through the use of databases such as Geographic Information Systems (GIS); use capabilities shared with other Service offices (e.g., Realty, LMVJV) whenever practical.
- Continue to develop GIS data layers depicting occurrence/abundance of plant and animal species (e.g., roost sites, vegetation cover maps) and management activities (e.g., forest management compartments, water management units).
- Coordinate with AGFC, USGS, COE, NRCS, and other organizations to design and conduct research that will provide refuge managers with information needed to improve habitat management programs to better fulfill refuge purposes.

RESOURCE PROTECTION

Bald Knob NWR Goal 3: Promote communication, cooperation, and partnerships between local, state, and federal agencies, land managers, and private citizens to minimize impacts from external habitat degradation and other threats to the functions and values of the refuge's associated wetland ecosystems and watersheds.

Discussion: In order to achieve its purposes and vision, Bald Knob NWR must address a number of issues that threaten to degrade or diminish the value of its resources. These threats include invasive plant and animal species, water quality and contaminant issues, development, and law enforcement.

Bald Knob NWR Objective 3-1: Invasive Plant and Nuisance Animal Control

Annually identify and eradicate or control invasive, exotic, or nuisance plants and animals, and develop and implement a database to systematically track occurrences and treatments within 2 years of the date of this CCP.
Discussion: Invasive plant species threaten refuge flora and fauna. Problems include European or Chinese privet and Japanese honeysuckle invasions along forest edges and in reforestation sites and some harvested stands, invasions of mimosa, chinaberry, and non-native pine in restored fields, and American lotus (although native) overtaking refuge impoundments.

Although beavers are a native species, their dam building activity and resulting flooding can interfere with intended habitat management on the refuge. Historically, beaver impoundments served to provide needed wetland habitat utilized by a variety of fauna. However, the surrounding watershed has changed and is now mostly agricultural instead of forested. Increased agricultural runoff, especially continual irrigation runoff during the growing season, has compounded the problem of beaver impoundments. Considerable staff time and funds are devoted to removing impoundments and controlling beaver populations.

Currently, trapping is prohibited on the refuge, but management should have the option of implementing a nuisance animal or furbearer management trapping program if necessary in the future. Nuisance animal removal should target beaver, nutria, and muskrat that negatively impact habitat and property, as well as predators such as raccoon, skunk, opossum, coyote, or bobcat that reduce priority wildlife populations and can pose disease risks. Similarly, night hunting of some species may be biologically sound and necessary and therefore should never be regarded as unconditionally prohibited. These options and others for predator, parasite, or disease control should be incorporated into management plans as needed for biological and human safety concerns.

Strategies:

- Implement invasive species prevention and control programs in compliance with 50 CFR 29.1 and EO 13112.
- Document occurrences of invasive plants and animals in a database developed during the course of the normal FHMP evaluation cycle and supplement the database with occurrences found during the course of normal management activities.
- Eradicate small plant infestations on the spot; when large infestations are encountered, develop and implement plans for coordinated control efforts.
- Control beaver populations through shooting and trapping and removal of impoundments.
- Develop and implement a database to track beaver kills and impoundment locations and characteristics.
- Consider allowing trapping/dispatching of beavers and other injurious/nuisance animals (e.g., nutria, muskrat, raccoon, skunks, opossums, feral hogs, and coyotes) conducted under special use permits issued to selected individuals, or by commercial trapping through quota special use permits to control exotic, invasive, or nuisance wildlife to protect refuge infrastructure, wildlife habitats, priority wildlife species, and prevent disease outbreaks.
- Document results and effects of treatment efforts and adjust accordingly (adaptive management).
- Continue to pursue grants to fund control activities.

Bald Knob NWR Objective 3-2: Water Quality

Continue to implement management actions to protect and improve quality of aquatic habitats on the refuge for the benefit of associated fish and wildlife resources.

Discussion: Turbidity and siltation of watercourses are the refuge's main water quality problems. Most of the overall problem is due to erosion and runoff (e.g., non-point sources) originating outside the refuge's boundaries. Illegal dumping of saltwater, toxins, chemicals, sludge, and drilling mud, resulting from oil and gas operations upstream of the refuge in the Overflow and Mingo Creek and Little Red River drainages, could become a problem in the future.

Strategies:

- Identify, assess, and treat areas prone to soil erosion prior to the development of sediment input problems, especially on recent acquisitions of prior-converted farmlands.
- Avoid increased siltation by following Best Management Practices (BMPs) for all refuge actions including farming, moist-soil management, construction, and road maintenance.

- Be alert to upstream activities causing problems in refuge waters (e.g., natural gas production) and develop a monitoring system to document potential water quality problems including sampling factors such as water and sediments, fish tissues, and rapid bio-assessment techniques.
- Where and when possible, allow natural stream flow processes and stream course changes to occur; if bank stabilization is necessary employ bioengineering techniques where feasible.
- To aid in soil stabilization within the context of the refuge's reforestation programs, plant appropriate species for hydrologic conditions of the treated site using flood-tolerant shrub and tree species such as common buttonbush (*Cephalanthus occidentalis*), black willow (*Salix nigra*), red maple (*Acer rubrum*), and baldcypress (*Taxodium distichum*) in the riparian corridor of prior-converted farmlands and other areas that are prone to erosion.
- Within the context of the refuge's reforestation and forest management plans, develop beaver population objectives for refuge lands and, as appropriate, manage beaver impoundments to contribute to refuge water quality goals and objectives.
- Document the location of all culverts and water control structures on the refuge, especially those repeatedly plugged by beavers. Where feasible and desirable, replace them with rock-lined fiords (low water crossings) to maintain vehicular access, discourage dam construction by beavers, reduce blockage of structures by debris, and facilitate suitable water movement.
- Work with Service private lands biologists, AGFC, Arkansas Natural Resources Commission (ANRC), ADEQ, and NRCS to develop incentives for local farmers and land owners that encourage the use of filter strips to limit agricultural runoff into adjacent waters.
- Recruit a Hydrologist based at Big Lake NWR to coordinate hydrological and water quality issues on all refuges within the Complex, coordinate hydrological research and monitoring, provide technical advice to adjacent landowners, provide liaison function with COE, and coordinate aquatic restoration projects.

Bald Knob NWR Objective 3-3: Contaminants

Determine if any contaminants exist on Bald Knob NWR, assess their impacts to the refuge, and appropriately mitigate these impacts.

Discussion: Level I Contaminants Surveys are done for each tract of land prior to acquisition. Level II surveys have been done for a couple of tracts that had previous petroleum products onsite or pesticide mixing activities. These or higher level contaminants surveys will be conducted for future acquisitions as the situation demands.
A study of potential chemical contaminant exposure and the biological effects of this exposure at 26 national wildlife refuges in the LMRE was conducted between 1995 and 2000 (Shea et al. 2001). Water, sediment, fish, and passive sampling devices were used to acquire toxicity data to characterize chemical exposure. The study also assessed the potential biological effects of this exposure. The primary focus of the study was on organochlorine pesticides, currently used pesticides, and mercury. Additional analyses were conducted for polychlorinated biphenyls and polycyclic aromatic hydrocarbons.

Organochlorine pesticides, such as DDT and toxaphene, were widely used for many years but were banned many years ago in the United States due to their persistence and tendency to bioaccumulate and biomagnify to levels that caused documented impacts on fish-eating birds such as Bald Eagles, Ospreys, and Brown Pelicans. Total DDT in sediment for Bald Knob NWR was less than the probable effect concentration.

At least two of the 50 current use pesticides measured – trifluralin and azinphos methyl – were detected at the refuge. Also detected were 2, 4-D, bentazon, metolachlor, and trifluralin. Concentrations of PCBs in fish, water and sediment were below known threshold levels for biological effects and water quality guidelines. Mercury was detected at the refuge in every fish, but concentrations were below thresholds for fish-eating mammals, and below levels that would cause concern over human health. No fish consumption advisories for mercury or other contaminants have been issued for water bodies on or flowing through Bald Knob NWR.

In conclusion, the contaminant study indicated that potential hazards for organochlorine pesticides, PBCs, polycyclic aromatic hydrocarbons, and mercury at Bald Knob NWR were unlikely. The potential hazard for current use pesticides was uncertain.

Strategy:

- Coordinate with personnel at the Service's Arkansas Ecological Services Field Office, ADEQ, and USGS to establish and maintain a contaminants and water quality monitoring program on the refuge, conduct surveys every five years or as necessary to assess containments that could affect the refuge's fish and wildlife, and document status and trends of the refuge's aquatic resources from the biological and physical perspectives.

Bald Knob NWR Objective 3-4: Land Acquisition

Acquire lands from willing sellers within or adjacent to the approved acquisition boundary of the refuge to enhance conservation programs, achieve legislated purposes of the refuge, and fulfill the mission of the Refuge System.

Discussion: The highest priority for land acquisition at Bald Knob NWR is the purchase of 19 inholdings. Several landowners of inholdings have even suggested the idea of trading. Potential human activities or development within these inholdings could be very detrimental to the creation and maintenance of a sanctuary area for waterfowl on surrounding refuge lands. The existing situation of allowing ingress/egress through the heart of the refuge to several inholdings already is a source of operational concern for the refuge. Realty specialists should immediately approach these private landowners and begin negotiations for appraisal and purchase. The most important tract of land is an 80-acre inholding within the waterfowl sanctuary on the south end of the refuge. The Service has the "right of first refusal" but progress has been slow on acquiring this tract.

The current acquisition boundary for the refuge encompasses 16,100 acres. Unfortunately, the acquisition boundary does not include some key areas with potential willing sellers and lands of high conservation values that would enable strategic growth of the refuge. From the landscape conservation perspective, there is a need to move the existing acquisition boundary to the north of the existing north boundary of the Mingo Creek Unit to encompass the floodplain of Mingo Creek and Cypress Slough. This minor boundary expansion of 1,610 acres would allow conservation and restoration of a significant wetland habitat corridor between Henry Gray/Hurricane Lake WMA and the Mingo Creek Unit of Bald Knob NWR on the local scale. On a regional scale, it would enhance the conserved habitat corridor from the Cache River/White River/Little Red River floodplain to the Ozark foothills. Additionally, greater protection would be afforded to the Mingo Creek wetlands and ongoing stream restoration efforts would be facilitated on the refuge. This expansion also would increase connectivity between the refuge and the WMA and provide additional opportunities for wildlife-dependent recreation. Furthermore, this expansion would facilitate acceptance of mitigation properties resulting from mitigation required for off-refuge impacts to wetlands associated with installation of the Fayetteville Express Natural Gas Pipeline slated to be installed in 2010. The refuge has already been approached by the environmental consultant for the gas company about its willingness to receive properties for inclusion in the refuge.

On a greater strategic landscape conservation scale, the Service also should consider further expanding the refuge's acquisition boundary north from the Mingo Creek Unit to create at least a 5,000-acre block along Mingo Creek to establish a large corridor between the Farm Unit of Bald Knob NWR and the adjacent 17,000-acre Henry Gray/Hurricane Lake WMA. Lands purchased in the major acquisition boundary expansion (from willing sellers) would be restored to a predominately hardwood forest. The product of acquisition, reforestation, and restoration would be a 22,000-acre contiguous block of bottomland hardwoods that would support not only key forest-breeding bird groups, such as Prothonotary Warblers, Northern Parula, Yellow-billed Cuckoo, and Wood Thrush, but also would have potential for waterfowl use if provisions are made to simulate occasional fall/winter flooding of bottomland forests in alternate three to four year periods. This expansion would benefit other indigenous bottomland hardwood forest species, such as Wood Ducks and American Woodcock, and would increase opportunities for compatible wildlife-dependent public use, including environmental education and interpretation.

An Environmental Assessment or Environmental Impact Statement would be conducted before acquiring any lands outside the approved acquisition boundary.

Strategies:

- Enable conservation, restoration, and management of additional wildlife and aquatic habitats on Bald Knob NWR through actively pursuing acquisition of lands from willing sellers.
- Pursue a minor boundary expansion (1,610 acres) along the Mingo Creek and Cypress Slough drainage north of the Mingo Creek Unit to create additional forest and wetland restoration opportunities for the benefit of trust species.
- Consider the feasibility and desirability of pursuing a major boundary expansion, particularly north of the Mingo Creek Unit, to form a corridor between the foothills of the Ozark Mountains to AGFC's Henry Gray/Hurricane Lake WMA covering approximately 40,000 acres.

Bald Knob NWR Objective 3-5: Cultural Resources

Within 10 years of the date of this CCP, develop and implement a Cultural Resources Management Plan.
Discussion: Refuge management will protect cultural resources in accordance with federal and state historic preservation legislation and regulations. To date, no cultural resources surveys or inventories have been conducted at Bald Knob NWR.

Strategies:

- Prepare a Cultural Resources Management Plan (CRMP) for the refuge.
- As guided by the CRMP:

- Conduct a Phase I archaeological survey of the non-flooded areas of the refuge by qualified personnel as a necessary first step in cultural resources management;
- Conduct a Phase II investigation if archaeological resources are identified during the Phase I survey, to determine the eligibility of identified resources for listing on the National Register of Historic Places prior to any disturbance;
- Conduct a Phase III data recovery if the resources identified in Phases I and II are determined to be eligible in order to recover data and mitigate the adverse effects of any undertaking;
- Follow procedures detailed in the CRMP for inadvertent discoveries of human remains;
- Ensure archaeological and cultural values are described, identified, and taken into consideration prior to implementing undertakings.
- Follow procedures outlined in the CRMP for consultation with the Service's Regional Historic Preservation Office, the State Historic Preservation Office, and potentially interested American Indian tribes.
- Develop a step-down plan for surveying lands to identify archaeological resources and for developing a preservation program.

VISITOR SERVICES

Bald Knob NWR Goal 4: Develop compatible, wildlife-dependent recreational programs that lead to enjoyable experiences, a greater understanding of fish, wildlife, and habitat conservation, and a greater appreciation for the value of Bald Knob NWR.

Discussion: Bald Knob NWR supports each of the priority public uses of national wildlife refuges as identified in the Improvement Act. These are hunting, fishing, wildlife observation, wildlife photography, and environmental education and interpretation. The primary public uses of the refuge are hunting and fishing. A large portion of the refuge is a waterfowl sanctuary that is closed to the public from November 15 to February 28. There are tremendous waterfowl and shorebird/wading bird populations on the refuge during the fall and winter months.

In addition to the efforts of the current visitor services program, the refuge will strive to promote birding and wildlife observation, provide information to visitors about contacting staff when the office is closed during regular business hours, and provide additional interpretive signage at various locations on the refuge. There is no visitor services specialist assigned to the refuge.

Bald Knob NWR Objective 4-1: Visitor Services Plan and Public Use Management

Continue to promote and manage appropriate and compatible public uses, and prepare and implement a Visitor Services Plan within 6 years of the CCP completion.

Discussion: The refuge does not have a current Visitor Services Plan. This step-down management plan will provide guidance for all of refuge management's efforts and programs on behalf of public visitation. This plan will improve the ability of staff to provide the visiting public with compatible opportunities to enjoy and appreciate fish, wildlife, plants, and other resources. As a result, the visiting public will develop an understanding and will build an appreciation of each individual's role in the environment, and in particular wildlife conservation, today and into the future.

All existing public uses occurring on the refuge have been evaluated for appropriateness. All activities have also been determined to be one of the six priority public uses, to support one of the priority public uses, or are wildlife-dependent. All visitor services activities are compatible with refuge purposes, goals, and objectives.

Strategies:

- Recruit a park ranger (Visitor Services specialist) to develop and implement a visitor services program on Bald Knob NWR.
- Develop a Visitor Services Plan (with public and partner involvement) that addresses the current and future recreation needs of refuge visitors and associated visitor services, including opportunities for mobility-impaired visitors; reflects applicable legislation, Service and Refuge System missions, directives, and policies; and supports refuge goals and objectives.
- The plan will specify programs for each type of public use, propose new facilities, address maintenance, upkeep, replacement, and/or elimination of current facilities, and identify a prospective timeline for implementation.
- Ensure that all compatibility determinations are re-evaluated as necessary.
- Maintain prohibition on camping.
- Restrict all-terrain vehicle (ATV) access to designated travel corridors only, monitor ATV access to ensure that it does not conflict with other uses, and allow ATVs only to directly support hunting.

Bald Knob NWR Objective 4-2: Visitor Welcome and Orientation

Implement visitor welcoming and orientation recommendations of the Bald Knob NWR Visitor Services Review Report according to the staggered timeframe (now, intermediate, and long-term) as outlined in that document.

Discussion: There are three main refuge entrance signs, all of which are main access points. One is located on Coal Chute Road, one on Safley Road, and one on Lone Star Road. Kiosks are also located at these locations. These kiosks offer hunting and fishing regulations and a refuge map. Directional signs are located on major road ways leading to main access points. Regulatory signs mark the seasonal waterfowl sanctuary boundary. A hunting brochure with annual regulations is available at the kiosks, headquarters, upon request by phone as well as on the website.

Presently, Bald Knob NWR does not have visitor facilities such as public restrooms or a regularly opened visitor contact station. Public roads are maintained but not marked with traffic control or directional signs. Parking lots are adequate for level of use through most of the year, with the exception of opening days of squirrel and muzzleloader deer seasons at the Mingo Creek Unit. Some unimproved roads must be closed due to heavy rains throughout the year.

The general leaflet is available at headquarters, kiosks, and upon request. No accessible alternatives exist for visitors with visual disabilities. The refuge does not have an audio-visual program nor does it have plans to develop one since there is no facility suitable for such use. The refuge now has a 3-person staff consisting of a refuge manager, engineering equipment operator, and park ranger (law enforcement – hired December 2008). The refuge manager interacts with the public and provides customer service. The public can usually reach a refuge employee by calling the Bald Knob NWR number, or can call Cache River NWR to receive information. Staff members wear the uniform properly and can be identified by such attire.

The current refuge office at Bald Knob NWR is a single-wide trailer that is not suitable for visitor reception and any type of environmental education or interpretive activities. The trailer is not fully accessible at the entrance or the inside. The trailer is unsightly due to its condition and appearance and is uninviting to the public. Funding has been obtained through the Amercian Reinvestment and

Recovery Act (ARRA) for replacement of the existing office with a suitable facility to allow for efficient public use management and administration of a visitor services program, including opportunities for environmental education and interpretation. The proposed headquarters/visitor contact station would be 1-story, approximately 2,500 square feet in size, fully ADA-compliant, and would include an exhibit area, volunteer/receptionist area, conference room, break room, law enforcement storage, public restrooms, staff offices, and public parking. This facility would be constructed within 75 yards of the current office site in the existing office/shop complex grounds, and thus would not result in loss of wildlife habitat. The new building would incorporate energy and resource conserving features that would reduce carbon and climate impacts.

Strategies:

- Replace the existing refuge office with a 2,500-square-foot headquarters/visitor contract station, using ARRA funding (approximately $650,000) and incorporating green-building design features to provide adequate facilities to meet the expectations and needs of the visiting public, to conduct visitor services programs, to facilitate work with partners, and to enable refuge staff to administer public use programs and associated operations.
- Place directional/road signs at road intersections within the Farm Unit, if necessary, upon development of an auto-tour route.
- Use traffic safety and information signs where appropriate.
- Provide universally accessible parking spots by adding signage and installing concrete pads in all established parking areas.
- Place a directional sign to the Mingo Creek Unit on Hurricane Lake Road before the turn at the bait shop.
- Post the office hours at the refuge headquarters.
- Consider methods to make kiosks more inviting to the public (e.g., using a different color scheme, a banner with the refuge name, a color map of the refuge with "you are here" notations, and enhanced lighting, if feasible).
- Ensure that refuge brochures, maps, and other visitor services products are up-to-date and readily available to the public.
- On the refuge website, use pictures that are most relevant to the refuge and add captions for the pictures, and post a calendar of events that includes significant wildlife viewing opportunities.

Bald Knob NWR Objective 4-3: Hunting

Annually provide and expand quality, compatible hunting opportunities as feasible.

Discussion: Biologically sound hunting is a legitimate activity on a national wildlife refuge and is one of the six priority public uses identified in the Improvement Act to be allowed, as long as it is found to be compatible with refuge purposes. Bald Knob NWR is relatively new and was opened to hunting in 1997 for small game, waterfowl, turkey, and deer. The refuge is open to small game hunting with squirrel and rabbit season largely following the state framework and bag limits. Non-toxic shot is required for shotguns and dogs are permitted for squirrel and rabbit hunting beginning December 1. Quail season also follows the state's framework and dogs are allowed on the refuge all season. Raccoon and opossum season runs for two weeks normally during the latter part of November. Dogs are required for the night hunting of raccoon. Pleasure running and field trials with dogs are prohibited. Furbearer trapping is prohibited. Access to the refuge is by automobile, ATV, boat, bicycle, and walking. All vehicles, including ATVs and bicycles, are restricted to designated roads, levee tops, and parking areas. Horses are prohibited. Public access to hunt areas may be closed at any time necessary to protect refuge resources or visitors.

Waterfowl hunting for both ducks and geese runs concurrent with the state seasons and bag limits. Retriever dogs are allowed for waterfowl hunting. However, many refuge-specific regulations impose further restrictions on waterfowl hunters. Hunter conflicts have been minimized by the implementation of the refuge-specific regulations. Currently, there are no major problems and most hunters are aware of all regulations and abide by those regulations.

Bald Knob NWR experiences large fluctuations in the number of duck hunters from year to year as well as within years. Availability of flooded habitat is the major factor that influences hunting pressure on the refuge. When parts of the state are extremely dry, there could be up to 150 waterfowl hunters each day for several days on Bald Knob NWR. However, when the White, Cache, and other major rivers are at flood stage, creating thousands of acres of waterfowl habitat and dispersing hunters, the number of hunters utilizing the refuge is general low, with as few as 20. As with most public hunting areas, the quality and success of a hunt are inversely proportional to the number of hunters utilizing the refuge.

The hunting area on Bald Knob NWR is over four miles wide, making ATVs a practical method to transport hunters and their gear to the various fields and woods, while reducing damage to levee tops that would result if trucks were allowed during this time of year. Currently, waterfowl hunters are allowed to enter and scout in the hunting area on ATVs in the afternoons. Additionally, small game and archery deer hunters enter this area to gain access to hunt areas. However, management concerns about waterfowl disturbance associated with these activities have prompted managers to consider modifying this practice, based on the following information.

Three seasons of waterfowl survey data (2006-07, 2007-08, 2008-09) were collected on Bald Knob NWR at least once every two weeks from noon (when hunting ends) to 4:00 p.m. from November to March. Waterfowl counts were conducted in fields within the Farm Unit. Estimated waterfowl numbers were compiled by species and impoundment. Waterfowl numbers estimated on afternoons following hunts were compared to waterfowl numbers estimated on afternoons during days in which no hunting occurred. Additionally, waterfowl numbers estimated on afternoons during a non-hunting split (the non-hunting period between open seasons during the waterfowl hunt year) were compared to numbers estimated during the afternoons of the next hunt day on which a survey was conducted (2007-08 and 2008-09 seasons only).

Although statistical analyses were not performed, bird use was higher on nearly every impoundment in the hunt area on afternoons of non-hunt days versus hunt days. Furthermore, estimated total bird use for the non-hunt split days was markedly higher than that of the following hunt days on which surveys were conducted. These results indicate that morning hunting contributes to decreased afternoon waterfowl use; however, other factors such as daily afternoon disturbance also may contribute to reduced afternoon bird use during the hunt days. Although waterfowl hunting ends at noon, hunters have until 1:00 p.m. to gather their gear and depart the area. Small game and archery deer hunters, as well as the general public, are allowed entry into the hunt area after 1:00 p.m. until dark by use of ATVs or by walking to scout for waterfowl hunting spots or otherwise to observe waterfowl and other wildlife. This activity has been allowed since 1997. General observations indicate that this activity results in additional waterfowl disturbance throughout the hunt area, as well as the areas of the waterfowl sanctuary that border the access roads to the hunt area. This frequent and repetitive disturbance contributes to increased energy expenditures and prevents waterfowl from using these areas for feeding, resting, and roosting. These combined effects decrease habitat suitability and hunt opportunity.

Refuge managers are considering implementing a trial "minimal disturbance zone," encompassing approximately 2,200 acres, in the core waterfowl hunting area by prohibiting all public entry and use into this zone after 1:00 p.m. from November 15 through February 28 (Figure 7). Only the North Granary Road public access via Frackin and Coal Chute Roads would remain open within this core area after 1:00 p.m. Other roads and portions of the hunting area would continue to be open after 1:00 p.m. for public ingress/egress by ATVs, motor vehicles, or pedestrians to allow access for afternoon archery deer and small game hunting, waterfowl scouting, and general wildlife observation and photography. Waterfowl surveys would be designed and implemented to characterize waterfowl use and determine whether afternoon scouting activity and/or other factors contribute to decreased waterfowl use and whether this public use management practice (1:00 p.m. closure) should be modified for better results, adopted permanently, or discontinued.

Also, in consideration of reducing waterfowl disturbance and improving waterfowl hunt quality, managers are considering modifying hunt access based on the following information. Designation of a "Walk-In Only" hunt area also may increase waterfowl use in the hunt area during afternoons and mornings. "Walk-In Only" hunting areas for target species such as wild turkeys, waterfowl, and deer are becoming increasingly common on federal and state wildlife management areas across the country. Walk-in hunt areas generally have less human noise, greater dispersion of hunters, fewer disturbances to both wildlife and hunters, and increased wildlife use, and thus, increased hunter success or satisfaction. A limited-sized (approximately 1-square-mile) "Walk-In Only" waterfowl hunt area on Bald Knob NWR could reduce human disturbance, increase waterfowl numbers, and increase hunter success and satisfaction. Refuge managers are considering implementing a trial, walk-in only hunt area during the waterfowl hunt season on a portion of the Farm Unit hunt area during which bird use, hunting success, and hunter satisfaction could be monitored and analyzed to determine program effectiveness and desirability.

After this trial period, a decision on whether to retain the "Walk-In Only" area could be made. If permanently implemented, a "Walk-in Only" area would not reduce the size of the overall hunting area; it would just reduce ATV access to the specific walk-in hunt area. Access to the majority of the refuge's hunting area would remain unchanged, and this modification would provide for a more diverse public hunting opportunity, while not favoring any particular group of hunters.

Opportunities for limited youth hunts, to help continue traditional outdoor hunting activities, have increased extensively over the past decade. The refuge has provided youth waterfowl hunts since 1999 and they have been received enthusiastically.

The refuge offers archery, muzzleloader, and modern gun hunting for deer. The harvest limit is one deer, either-sex, per hunt except for the archery season in which the statewide bag limit of three applies. The total number of bucks that can be harvested through a combination of all refuge hunts is two. There are no antler restrictions for buck deer. The archery season runs concurrent with the state season. Typically, the archery season opens in October and closes at the end of February. The muzzleloading deer season lasts for 9 days and usually starts during the middle of October. It coincides with the state's first muzzleloading season.

Figure 7. Proposed Minimal Disturbance Zone for Waterfowl on Bald Knob NWR

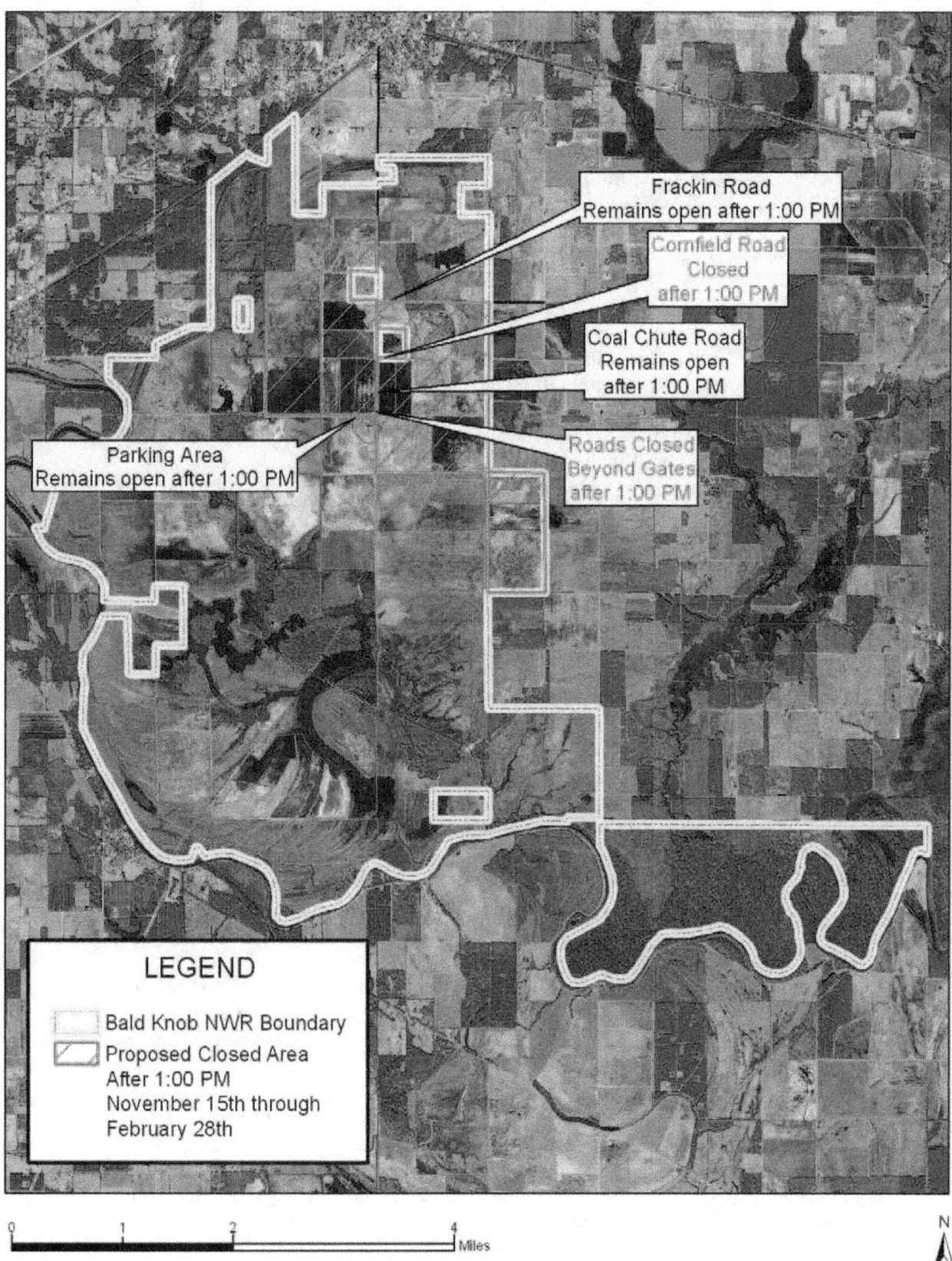

The refuge also has a 2-day youth deer modern gun hunt the first weekend in November and a 2-day Quota Gun Deer Hunt on the Farm Unit only, which falls on the opening weekend of the state's modern gun hunt, usually the second Saturday in November. Shotguns with rifled slugs, legal pistols, and muzzleloaders only may be possessed and used for these hunts. Hunters can harvest only one either-sex deer per hunt.

Fall archery Eastern Wild Turkey hunting is allowed only on the Mingo Creek Unit. The season runs concurrently with the archery deer season and the state bag limit applies. The season dates and bag limit runs concurrent with the state framework for Zone 4. Firearms are prohibited.

Although no specific seasons exist for these animals, hunters can take beaver, muskrat, nutria, coyote, feral hog, and armadillo during any refuge hunt by the use of the device appropriate for that hunt.

Strategies:

- Continue to conduct annual cooperative AGFC/refuge hunt regulation meetings and standardize regulations across Arkansas NWRs and State WMAs where and when feasible.
- Continue to restrict entry and disturbance in the waterfowl sanctuaries during the November 15 – February 28 closure.
- Consider implementing a "minimal disturbance zone" within the waterfowl hunt area from November 15 through February 28 by prohibiting public entry and use after 1:00 p.m. into a specified area (as depicted in Figure 7) to reduce disturbance to waterfowl and improve quality of (next day) waterfowl hunting.
- Consider implementing a walk-in hunting only hunting area in a portion of the waterfowl hunting area to reduce waterfowl disturbance and improve hunt quality.
- Allow ATV access for hunting only and restrict access to designated roads, levee tops, and parking areas. ATV access will be permitted only from September 1 to February 28.
- Mobility-impaired hunters may apply for a special use permit, allowing specialized access by ATV. Provide hunting opportunities for mobility-impaired hunters as feasible.
- Monitor ATV access and modify as needed to mitigate any negative impacts to refuge habitats, infrastructure, and visitors in compliance with Executive Orders 11644 and 11989
- Continue to maintain seasonal closed areas around eagle nests during the nesting season to reduce disturbance when and where necessary.
- Consider revising the refuge hunt brochure as follows:
  - Include a "quick reference chart" that lists all the hunts and dates.
  - Clarify that the refuge is closed to all other public entry and use during the Quota Gun Deer Hunt.
  - Stipulate the removal of flagging and reflective tacks at end of hunts.
- Create additional opportunities for big game hunters by expanding modern gun deer hunting if such action does not conflict with refuge purposes or other uses.
- Create additional opportunities for small game hunters by opening up dove, snipe, and woodcock hunting to statewide seasons if such action does not conflict with refuge purposes or other uses.
- Provide additional hunting areas/impoundments and improve water management throughout the refuge that would enhance hunting opportunities if feasible.
- Continue to allow Snow Goose hunting during the state conservation order hunting period.
- Consider reducing the deer muzzleloader season from 9 days to 5 days for consistency with Cache River NWR, if appropriate.
- Discontinue the spring archery turkey season on the Mingo Creek Unit.

- Continue expanding youth hunting opportunities if feasible, including allowing a limited spring youth gun turkey hunt in the Mingo Creek Unit that would correspond to the dates of the adjacent Hurricane Lake WMA youth turkey hunt.
- Utilize methods such as quotas, permits, hunt area zoning, or period limitations as warranted to maintain quality and safety of hunt activities.
- Periodically assess hunter satisfaction and quality of hunts (e.g., birds per hunter, hunter densities).
- Hire a full-time law enforcement officer to be stationed on Bald Know NWR, to provide more adequate visitor and resource protection and enforce laws and regulations (accomplished December 2008).

Bald Knob NWR Objective 4-4: Fishing

Annually provide and expand quality, compatible fishing opportunities as feasible.

Discussion: Sport fishing and frogging are permitted year-round in accordance with state regulations, except for the 6,000-acre waterfowl sanctuary that is closed to all public entry and use from November 15 through February 28. Approximately 14 miles of 20- 60-foot wide irrigation canals (6 feet deep), 100 miles of smaller ditches, and several cypress-tupelo brakes and oxbow lakes provide access for bank and boat fishing. Seven boat ramps developed and maintained by the Service provide access for fishing. The Liberty Valley ramp is of significant value as it is the only public ramp for approximately 12 river miles.

Refuge waters provide habitat for fish desired by anglers, such as crappie, bream, catfish, and bass. Other species caught include drum, carp, smallmouth buffalo, and gar. Natural stocking occurs from the Little Red River through a large flood-control structure on Overflow Creek. Fish populations within the canals, ditches, and brakes are self-sustaining through natural reproduction.

The best fishing opportunities are from March-June, and at night during summer months. Water control structures throughout the levee and canal system often produce flowing water, resulting in increased catch potential. The new Concrete Dam, Mingo Creek, and Jim Wright Pond also provide good fishing opportunities. Bow fishing is allowed and occurs in very limited numbers. No special permit is required for fishing in refuge waters.

At the present time, fishing pressure is moderate, and user conflicts have not been apparent. One issue that needs to be addressed is littering by bank fishermen. Due to minimal staffing, including only one collateral duty officer, patrols and enforcement of the fishing program are limited (a full-time law enforcement officer was hired December 2008).

Strategies:

- Revise the fishing section in the annual public use, hunting, and fishing brochure to improve readability.
- Develop an accessible fishing facility at an appropriate site on the refuge, if feasible.
- Work with Service fisheries biologists to improve the refuge's fish and aquatic habitats.
- Modify fishing access during the critical waterfowl wintering period if necessary to reduce disturbance impacts to migratory birds.
- Monitor frog populations and consider reducing bag limit and/or season length to prevent overharvest.

Bald Knob NWR Objective 4-5: Wildlife Observation and Photography

Annually provide and expand quality, compatible wildlife observation and photography opportunities as feasible.

Discussion: Access to the refuge for wildlife observation and photography is typically allowed during daylight hours year-round on more than 80 miles of gravel roads and levees within the Farm Unit. Passenger vehicles, bicycles, and walking are permitted. All vehicles, including bicycles, are restricted to designated roads, levee tops, and parking areas. An exception to open access is the 6,000-acre waterfowl sanctuary that is closed to all public entry and use from November 15 through February 28. Seven public boat ramps provide sites to launch boats into the Little Red River and various brakes for birding and wildlife observation. To protect refuge roads, gates are closed any time major flooding events occur or are anticipated. Horses/mules are prohibited year-round.

Diverse habitats create excellent opportunities for wildlife viewing and photography. Farm fields with varying crops, moist-soil impoundments, and reforested hardwood areas in various stages of growth, bottomland hardwood swamps, and cypress-tupelo brakes are all visible from the levee roads. White-tailed deer, river otters, bobcats, Eastern Wild Turkeys, numerous reptiles and amphibians, egrets, herons, and many songbirds are present year-round. During late summer and early fall, migrating shorebirds flock to the impounded areas by the tens of thousands to gather food for energy needed to complete their journeys. Fall brings as many as half a million ducks and geese: Blue, Snow, Canada, and White-fronted Geese feed in the stubble left from farming. Mallards, Northern Pintail, Blue and Green-winged Teal, and Wood Ducks feed and loaf in wetter areas during fall and winter months. Also during fall and winter, up to 60 Bald Eagles can be seen soaring across the fields and swamps. One Bald Eagle nest, visible with a spotting scope from the road, is located in a large cypress tree within the Pole Brake area. Many species of raptors including Peregrine Falcons, Red-shouldered Hawks, and Northern Harriers use refuge habitat for foraging.

Perhaps the most noticeable of wildlife during summer months are the songbirds. In the hardwood forests and swampy areas, songs of a dozen species of birds are easily heard at every stop. Indigo Buntings, White-eyed Vireos, Carolina Wrens, Tufted Titmouse, Yellow-billed Cuckoos, Acadian Flycatchers, Red-winged Blackbirds, Cardinals, Eastern Wood Peewees, and a variety of woodpeckers are among the more common.

Currently, no designated auto tour routes, observation platforms/blinds, or boardwalks exist on the refuge. A primitive 1.25-mile walking trail (one way) is located within the Squirrel Woods. Three kiosks, located at main entrances to the refuge, provide general refuge information including a list of allowed and prohibited activities. The refuge has low levels of use for wildlife observation and photography much of the year, with more moderate numbers during fall through late winter.

Issues of concern include littering, mudding (vehicular trespass off graveled roads and into farm fields, dirt roads, and levees during wet periods), vandalism of kiosks, signs, and permit boxes, tampering with water control structures, and some artifact collecting. The staff attributes these activities to the inadequate law enforcement coverage.

www.ingramcontent.com/pod-product-compliance
Lightning Source LLC
Chambersburg PA
CBHW052002280526
45793CB00005B/820